KT-170-741

Hibernian Greats

Hibernian Greats

STEWART BROWN

Foreword by

BERNARD GALLACHER

JOHN DONALD PUBLISHERS LTD
EDINBURGH

John Donald Publishers Ltd.,
138 St. Stephen Street, Edinburgh,
EH3 5AA.

ISBN 0 85976 192 4

ACKNOWLEDGEMENTS

My special thanks to the various individuals who gave up their time to reflect on great careers and to all others who contributed amusingly and shrewdly with their observations.

The co-operation of Mrs Carol Hamilton was much appreciated and I am indebted to golfer Bernard Gallacher for supplying the Foreword during his busiest period of the season.

Pictorially, the *Evening News* and *The Scotsman* kindly provided most of the illustrations. I am grateful to these newspapers and also to the *Daily Record* and *Daily Mail*.

Phototypeset by Newtext Composition Ltd., Glasgow.
Printed in Great Britain by Bell & Bain Ltd., Glasgow.

Foreword

January 1, 1960. The date is etched indelibly in my mind. For on that Ne'erday I made my debut as a 12 year old as a Hibs fan. It was the annual ritual against Hearts . . . and we lost SIX NIL!

Hardly the most encouraging start for any budding fan but as I travelled back to Bathgate by bus that gloomy afternoon my schoolboy logic told me: 'Why worry? things can only get better.' And I was right. That six nil defeat might have been hard to take but I was well and truly hooked. My love affair with Hibs had begun . . . and anyway five of the goals were offside!

And the love affair is still going strong . . . even though at times it's been rather a costly relationship. I often wonder how many pocketfuls of pesetas, escudos, francs and sterling I must have poured into telephone boxes all over Europe as I've phoned home to find out how Hibs have done on matchdays.

There have been disappointments, of course, but there have been magical moments too . . . training at Easter Road with that marvellous team of the seventies skippered by my all-time favourite, Pat Stanton, one of the greats featured in this book.

Those marvellous European nights under Jock Stein and Eddie Turnbull when featured players such as the late Willie Hamilton, then John Brownlie, tormented Europe's best.

The winning of the League Cup, the almost winning the Fairs Cup . . . and above all the knowledge that over the years, following in the tradition of the Famous Five, Easter Road has paraded players of quality.

This book honours nine of them: Gordon Smith, Lawrie Reilly, Tommy Younger, Joe Baker, Pat Stanton, Willie Hamilton, John Brownlie, George Best and Alan Rough.

I've been lucky enough to see most of them play and I'm sure, like me, you'll enjoy re-living some of their greatest moments as Hibs players.

Remembering their exploits even made me forget January 1 1960 . . . for a while!

Bernard Gallacher

Contents

Introduction

Selecting a handful of individuals for inclusion in a 'Hall of Fame' is a matter of personal choice and a difficult one when scores of great players have worn the famous green and white of Hibs in the club's long and illustrious history.

But in sticking to players I have known personally and admired from Gordon Smith to Alan Rough, the book covers a period of more than 40 years and highlights the deeds of men who excelled for club and country.

Gordon Smith, the most gifted; Lawrie Reilly the most capped and tenacious; and cat-like goalkeeper Tommy Younger take us through the war years to the marvellous side which won three championships in five years, and a bit further on.

Joe Baker, who made history in being selected for England when he craved to be a Scot; the mercurial Willie Hamilton; and team-mates Pat Stanton and John Brownlie, who shared in the last major trophy triumph, all justify inclusion.

Irishman George Best arrived to soften the torment of relegation for the supporters and pulled in crowds that were exceptional, and then Alan Rough came along to join a long line of distinguished goalkeepers, having become the most honoured Scot in his position.

There may be dissenting voices as to why someone has been included or omitted and I can appreciate there will be many views other than mine.

I might have gone for Bobby Johnstone, Eddie Turnbull or Willie Ormond from the 'Famous Five' which was, without question, the best forward line that British football has seen since the Second World War. Or their ubiquitous colleague Bobby Combe, who filled in anywhere except goal and did a super job – the man with the billiard-table legs.

There was big Jock Govan, first of the overlapping full backs and far ahead of his time; Davie Shaw who formed an international full back partnership with his brother Jock, of Rangers; centre half Hugh Howie and even goalkeeper Jimmy Kerr, uncapped but so highly thought of by those who played in front of him.

Peter Cormack left to achieve success in Europe and England

under the direction of canny Bill Shankly at Liverpool, just as Des Bremner helped Aston Villa to follow their English League win with the Champions Cup.

The list of names is endless with Alex Cropley, Alex Edwards, Jim O'Rourke, Johnny MacLeod, John Blackley, Arthur Duncan, Jackie McNamara etc. holding a special place in the affections of those who followed them. If your personal favourite has been missed, accept my apology.

I have often thought it a sin that nobody bothered to put on record the exploits of Smith when lesser mortals had books written about them. Gordon captained Hibs and Scotland, won League badges with three different clubs and represented them all in the European Cup.

Perhaps a little of that damage may be repaired by giving him his rightful place in this publication among the greats who have graced Easter Road.

I derive pleasure from turning back the clock to compare the stars of yesteryear with the household names of today. Just imagine if it was possible to bring the best together in a modern squad that could look like this – Younger, Rough; Brownlie; Howie, Stanton, Blackley, Shaw; Smith, Combe, Johnstone, Reilly, Baker, Turnbull, Ormond and Best. Who would need a defence with that class of attacking stars?

Of course, Hibs have been producing characters and personalities since the club was founded by Irish immigrants in 1875. It transpires that Mick Whelahan, the first captain and an antecedent of Pat Stanton, sometimes played in goal, on other occasions at centre forward or where he was needed.

Hibs became the first Edinburgh club to win the Scottish Cup in 1887 though not without considerable drama. After they had beaten Vale of Leven 3-1 in the semi final, the losers lodged a protest with the SFA, claiming that Hibs were paying a player.

All clubs had been warned that expulsion would be the penalty for illegal payments and that players in receipt of cash would be banned for two years.

The SFA decided to delay the inquiry until the final was decided and Hibs beat Dumbarton 2-1 to collect the trophy.

It was only on the morning of the final that Hibs discovered the probe concerned star player Willie Groves who was supposed to be receiving £1 weekly in lieu of lost time at the factory where he worked.

Vale had been tipped off by one of Groves' workmates but it didn't stop him from starring in the final. Wild celebrations went on and no thought was given to the possibility of losing the Cup. On the following Tuesday, it was the casting vote of the chairman which sanctioned their victory on insufficient evidence.

Hibs won what was billed as a 'world championship match' against Preston before Groves was one of four players who defected to the newly formed Celtic. Subsequently, Hibs went defunct for a few years, and the club was resurrected as a non-sectarian outfit.

Goalkeeper Harry Rennie, frequently positioned on the halfway line, was one of the famous members of the notable team at the turn of the century and Paddy Callaghan was another in Dan McMichael's side.

Hibs beat Rangers at Ibrox with 10 men for part of the game and mastered Celtic on their own ground by a McGeechan goal to lift the Scottish Cup in 1902. They crushed Celtic 6-2 in the Glasgow Charity Cup for good measure and went on to become champions in the following season when they had six points to spare from Dundee.

Personalities abounded in the team which lost in the Scottish Cup final in 1923 and 1924. There was inside forward Jimmy Dunn, who became one of the Wembley Wizards, and centre forward Jimmy McColl, most of whose life was devoted to Hibs.

Before coming to Easter Road he scored twice to beat Hibs in the 'Scottish' final of 1914 and left Celtic six years later for Stoke because he wasn't permitted to join a Scottish club. However, he came home to Partick Thistle and Hibs boss Alex Maley signed the little Glaswegian.

Jimmy scored 130 goals and then had a shot at managing Belfast Celtic. He returned to Hibs as assistant trainer, moved up as Hugh Shaw took over the managership and spent the rest of his days at the ground even after his retiral.

He was never without a cheroot, had a shrewd eye for a player and lived into his 80s. Gordon Smith was his favourite and he wouldn't hear of any comparison with Stanley Matthews, but Jimmy also told me: 'I've known all the good ones . . . Cunningham, McMenemy and Gallacher but I never saw a finer inside forward than Bobby Johnstone.'

Hibs presented Jimmy with an inscribed gold watch in 1971 at the age of 78 to mark their appreciation of his services.

Willie Harper was the goalkeeper in the '20s team, an ex-

Guardsman, blacksmith and boxer – an awesome sight for opponents and an inspiration to his own team.

He belonged to Lanarkshire, played junior football with Edinburgh Emmet and spent five years with Hibs before going to Arsenal for a similar period. His next stop was Plymouth where he was player, trainer and odd-job man looking after the laundry for more than 40 years.

Willie, who never played in a losing Scotland team in four matches against England, started the fashion of yellow jerseys for goalkeepers. They wore grey or brown until Harper decided to brighten his appearance, and it was an innovation that caught on.

Whatever Hibs have been good at over the years, their record in Scottish Cup finals is astonishingly poor, allowing for some bad breaks along the way. As I've pointed out, they were second best in 1914, 1923, 1924, 1947, 1958, 1972 and 1979. Seven in a row, and it hasn't mattered who has been in charge.

Hibs have had 12 managers since the end of the Second World War. The flamboyant Willie McCartney, the inevitable carnation in his buttonhole, was the only one I never met. He was installed pre-war and fashioned a team to become champions just a few months after his death in 1948.

McCartney believed in the policy of signing 20 young players to unearth one star, and the system worked in that Hugh Shaw inherited a great side when he moved off the trainer's bench.

'Shoo Shaw,' as chairman Harry Swan seemed to refer to him, had played in the outstanding team of the mid-20s, and the stooped ex-wing half occupied the managerial chair until the end of 1961. To a young reporter, he was an aloof man with a curious habit of wearing braces outside his pullover.

Walter Galbraith succeeded him and introduced a string of unknowns from English football where he had managed Tranmere. But the former full back, who could have doubled for Douglas Fairbanks jnr, bought good players, too, such as Neil Martin, Willie Hamilton and Pat Quinn.

The Tranent-born Neil proved a £7000 bargain and Galbraith signed him from Queen of the South just as the big forward threatened to take up lorry-driving and quit the game.

Walter also took physiotherapist Tom McNiven to Easter Road for what turned into a 25-year stay on behalf of club and country. But the manager's sharp eye for quality didn't produce a smooth blend and Hibs diced dangerously with relegation in 1963.

Indeed, it took 4-0 away wins against Queen of the South and Raith Rovers in the last two League matches to leave Clyde and Raith as the drop-outs.

Jock Stein arrived in 1964 for a short but memorable period in which he raised the fans' hopes of a League and Cup double only to be spirited away to his beloved Celtic before either competition could be completed.

There is no saying what he might have done at Easter Road because Jock had saved Dunfermline from apparently certain relegation and led them to an amazing Scottish Cup success in the next season.

Stein was a marvellous manager during and after his spell with Hibs and an absolute dream for a journalist with his uncanny ability to see or manufacture stories.

He telephoned me early one morning at the office to ask the deadline for the last edition and then in that familiar gravel voice, Jock told me: 'You can prepare a story for the afternoon but don't print a line in the early editions.'

What was the cunning devil cooking up that demanded such secrecy? Quickly, he revealed the plot and said: 'I'm selling John Parke to Sunderland for £38,000 but before that deal goes through, Joe Davis is joining us from Third Lanark for £7000.'

'Bill Hiddleston (who ran Thirds) would be furious if he knew about the sale of Parke, so it's essential that nothing is said too soon.'

'Telephone me at Roker Park about three o'clock and I'll confirm that the business has been done.'

Sure enough, the twin transaction went through and he chuckled at what was my first experience of a manager buying first to sell at a profit.

He knew that I had recommended the Irish international left back to Hibs after seeing him play in separate representative games against Willie Henderson and Davie Wilson. Galbraith had suggested I might tell him about any useful players in the Irish sides and Parke cost them £12,000, on the day Bob Shankly tried to buy him for Dundee.

Stein added: 'It was too good an offer to turn down. We've bought a replacement and made a profit of more than £30,000.' Davis, in fact, proved a shrewd investment and was the king of penalty takers for some seasons.

Before Hibs met Real Madrid in a challenge match in October, 1964, Jock rubbed his hands gleefully and said: 'We've enough material to build up this game over a period of six weeks. I'll give you a story about the various conditions they're laying down every week.'

He was as good as his word and Hibs wore all-green in that game because Real insisted that only they should wear white!

Stein is the best manager I've dealt with and it was one of the saddest nights in my life when he died so suddenly at Ninian Park on September 10, 1985 after his two second-half substitutions had put Scotland on the road to the World Cup finals in Mexico.

Bob Shankly, on Stein's say-so, left Dundee for Hibs and didn't possess any of his predecessor's gift for story angles.

At first, when I interviewed him in his office at Dens Park, he struck me as an awkward customer. One foot resting on a chair, elbow on his knee and cigarette in hand in a characteristic pose, he was less than co-operative.

But, within a month, he began to show trust and it became evident that Bob was a straight guy. He had done extremely well in winning a championship at Dundee but was tired of selling players.

Predicting results was not his game except once when Hibs were beaten 4-1 in Naples and Colin Grant had missed a few chances. Immediately following that first-leg defeat in an afternoon game, he stated: 'They think it's all over but Hibs will beat them and qualify'. The over-confident Italians were thrashed 5-0 in Edinburgh.

Having played with the quaintly named Glenbuck Cherrypickers, he had a knack of producing the most unusual expressions. One night in the Volksparkstadion in Hamburg, he watched the squad lap the pitch and said of one player who had better be nameless: 'That yin runs like a pregnant ear-i-wig.'

However, there was no escape from selling players and the departure of Colin Stein to Rangers for £100,000 in November, 1968 was about the last straw for him. Stein thanked Hibs for his release by hitting a hat trick against them in his debut and, though Joe McBride was bought from Celtic and scored 13 goals in 10 games, Bob was disillusioned with football, and an attempt to quit was rejected.

Shankly bowed out the following September when Peter Cormack's two goals against St. Mirren let him leave on a winning note.

Willie Macfarlane, a former Hibs right back, breezed into the job with all the confidence in the world and made an instant hit with the fans by leading the team to victory at Tynecastle!

While he lasted only 15 months, Willie was involved in several deals. He bought Johnny Graham, Arthur Duncan and Erich Schaedler and sold Peter Marinello to Arsenal for £100,000 and Peter Cormack to Nottingham Forest for a bit less.

Marinello's transfer was supposed to be a secret and Willie wanted to avoid the media at the airport. He tried to sell a dummy to my late colleague John Ayres by asking a Turnhouse employee to tell him they were leaving the terminal building by a certain door – which was the wrong one.

But the story was all stitched up and Willie didn't realise there would be a photographer at the London end poised to wire a picture of their arrival.

Perth-born Dave Ewing joined the club as coach but a change of control at the top saw Tom Hart's regime thrust him into the managerial chair on the same day that Hibs were to face Liverpool in the Fairs Cup.

The likeable Ewing had departed within seven months and the way was clear to bring in Eddie Turnbull, who had been linked with the job for years whenever it became vacant.

It was at Gleneagles Hotel that he agreed to leave Aberdeen for what proved to be an eventful nine-year stint. Disappointment came early to him when Hibs were crushed 6-1 by Celtic in the final of the Scottish Cup in May, 1972.

Hibs had laid on a win-or-lose reception in the North British Hotel after the game and the champagne seemed rather flat and out of place. But Eddie swore to me in defeat: 'Mark my words, we'll beat them next time at Hampden.' And he fulfilled that promise.

Hibs beat them 5-3 in the Drybrough Cup in August and returned in December to lift the League Cup by a 2-1 margin. That post-final get-together was considerably cheerier and Hibs retained the Drybrough Cup against Celtic in the following season.

But Turnbull, who made brilliant use of substitutes in his early days, wanted a championship title and he thought the acquisition of Joe Harper would fulfil that ambition.

Hibs and Aberdeen kept outbidding one another for the Everton player and Tom Hart told the manager: 'If you are anxious to sign him, another £20,000 won't stop us.' So Hibs shelled out £120,000 not to mention VAT and Harper's cut.

It was a costly transaction in every way because Alex Cropley had to go south to balance the books.

The Harper transfer was concluded in a Carlisle hotel and it was puzzling why Joe kept on his heavy suede coat throughout the talks.

Perhaps he was conscious of being overweight but, whatever the reason, his signing was bad business.

Hibs had their most famous left-wing partnership together again once Willie Ormond had finished with Scotland and Hearts to become number two to Turnbull. But they were bad times at Easter Road as Hibs slid towards the First Division without a single away point.

Turnbull moved out and Ormond assumed charge in April, 1980 and began with a 1-1 draw at Aberdeen even if it was much too late to avoid relegation.

Willie was an extremely pleasant man. 'You wouldn't have heard of Pele if I'd possessed a right foot,' he used to joke. The wee Musselburgh man had Hibs on course for a fast return to the Premier League with a score of 24 points from 17 games, and then poor health forced him to resign to concentrate on his bar.

Bertie Auld, of the flat bunnets and mammoth cigars, brought his Glasgow humour to the Capital though the fans were not over-enamoured with his defensive ideals.

Tom Hart's death in March, 1982 was bad news for everyone and, in particular, Auld, Pat Quinn and John Lambie because the new chairman Kenny Waugh didn't fancy Bertie and there was a further change at the top in September.

It was a popular move to appoint Pat Stanton who had George Stewart and Jimmy O'Rourke as back-up men. But, after buying Alan Rough, he found there was no more money for players and packed up only to be persuaded to carry on.

A 3-2 home defeat by Dumbarton in September, 1984 and a running battle with the SFA persuaded him that he'd had enough. John Blackley took over to re-model the team which lost the League Cup final to Aberdeen in 1985.

Gordon Durie, whom he had signed for £65,000, was sold to Chelsea for a reported £400,000 (of which East Fife received a chunk) and Brian Rice went to Nottingham Forest for £175,000 – an inflated price fixed by a tribunal.

Blackley was allowed to spend the money but didn't use it wisely. Billy Kirkwood, Stuart Beedie, Mark Fulton, Mark Caughey were here-today, gone-tomorrow signings.

And now Alex Miller, a sincere, honest and hard-working boss is left with Peter Cormack to bring stability and success to the club that has gone through managers at a brisk rate since Turnbull's era.

Harry Swan, a baker to trade, was the chairman pre-war and

throughout the glory days. As a football visionary, he was in a class of his own and used to talk about floodlights, sponsorship and European competition long before he was instrumental in making them happen.

'Wee Harry' was the first SFA president from Easter Road and, though he had a reputation for selling, he managed to keep most of the outstanding players with the exception of Johnstone, who went to Manchester City.

Bookmaker Bill Harrower succeeded him as principal shareholder and was never happier than when Jock Stein managed the team. But there were Saturdays when he didn't bother about football and it seemed strange to own a club and not watch them!

Tom Hart was different once he bought the controlling interest. Lively, controversial and an out-and-out Hibs supporter, he insisted on the best for the club. He had become wealthy from selling his building company and ploughed money into the club which he later recouped.

Tom spoke fearlessly in fighting for Hibs' rights, a breath of air in Scottish football, and there was nobody more sincere.

He asked me to operate as the middleman when his health warned him that it was time to pass on the reins, and Kenny Waugh, another self-made individual with bookmaking and pub interests, came to terms for the club.

Kenny never tried to match Tom's ebullient style of leadership but preferred to put the housekeeping in order and to run the club on sound financial lines.

He altered the main terracing to give the stadium a more compact appearance and mastermind various structural alterations within the stand. Having been chairman since March, 1982, Kenny was approached at the end of last season about a take-over by David Duff, a 33 year old Edinburgh born solicitor based in Wiltshire.

Negotiations remained secret until July when it became known that David was prepared to buy the chairman's 406,000 shares for just over £700,000.

The ex-Trinity Academy scholar, a keen Hibs fan since he started school, has been enormously successful in business with interests in property, travel, furniture, an hotel, restaurant and mining equipment, and was anxious to bring his expertise and enthusiasm to Easter Road to enhance the fortunes of Hibs.

Gordon Smith

Gordon Smith stands out as the most revered and famous player in the club's history. A goalscoring cavalier of immense grace, elegance and skill who established football records unlikely to be equalled, let alone surpassed.

Those unfortunate followers who never saw the undisputed king of the wing in his 18 years with Hibs or shorter yet magical spells with Hearts and Dundee know about him because his legendary deeds have been passed down over the years.

He was often compared to those English wizards Stanley Matthews and Tom Finney but Gordon was the best of this trio and there is an interesting comment from that noted marksman, Jimmy Greaves, in a book about the game's most gifted goalscorers.

Gordon is referred to as 'one of Scotland's greatest wingers' and Greaves comments: 'I am reliably informed that at his peak he had the dribbling skill of Matthews and the shooting power and accuracy of Finney. He could not have a better dual rating.'

He captained Hibs and Scotland and was a perfectionist on the park, capable of dropping the ball on a colleague's head or at his feet from any range. And, unlike so many modern football stars, the 'Gay Gordon,' as he was affectionately known, had two good feet, pace and could score goals with his head.

In short, he had everything and that is why Gordon still enjoys the role of Easter Road idol. Two summers ago, he was a top table guest at a function in honour of Hibs physiotherapist, Tom McNiven, in the North British Hotel. To say he was given a rapturous reception by some 500 diners is an understatement and Gordon was the star of the night to these guests. He confessed later to me that he was astounded and humbled by the warmth of the welcome.

Gordon is the proud possessor of five championship badges, three won with Hibs and one each with Hearts and Dundee. That is an unique achievement and he represented all three teams in the European Cup, twice playing in semi finals.

There isn't another player past or present with that pedigree though he might have swopped one of those treasured league awards for one Scottish Cup badge. That was the honour which eluded Gordon and his 'Famous Five' mates but, of course, a medal from that competition has been unobtainable for thousands of Hibs players since the trophy was captured last in 1902.

His international career spanned 13 years, from a Wembley debut in war-time to his final appearance against Spain in a World Cup qualifying match in which he signed off with Scotland's only goal.

Willie Waddell was his big rival on the Scotland scene and Gordon readily admits that the Ibrox man was 'a much better internationalist' but the post-war records show that Smith won more caps than the Rangers winger – 18 to 17. Gordon also figured in three war-time matches, an unofficial international against South Africa and nine Inter League games.

He was abused by many defenders, suffered two leg breaks and a shattered ankle (which he jokes stopped him playing until he was 50) yet justified the remark by the late Wilson Strachan, former chairman of Hearts, who declared: "Gordon is the perfect gentleman on and off the field." Booked only three times in his life, he regards two of these cautions as being totally unfair but concedes the punishment was right for a retaliatory foul on ex-Rangers half back, Scot Symon.

Although Gordon was born in Edinburgh, the Smith family moved to Montrose when he was an infant and it was in the minor grades in Angus that he took the first steps to fame – and how close Hibs were to losing him to Hearts at the age of 16.

He became a schoolboy internationalist at Montrose Academy, played for a team called Bromford in Arbroath and felt that real progress was being made when, at 14, he joined Kirriemuir Harp. The next step was into the junior grade with Montrose Roselea and a match fee of half a crown signalled his professionalism.

Gordon had moved on to Dundee North End when he was selected to play for a Junior XI against a Hearts-Hibs Select to mark the opening of the new Lochee Harp ground at Beechwood Park. He scored a hat trick against Bobby Baxter to pull off a 3-2 win.

Says Gordon: 'When I read the newspapers the following day, I thought I was on my way to Hearts and that was great because I supported them at that time. After all, I was Edinburgh-born and felt entitled to follow a team from the city.'

'Hearts had famous players like Walker and Massie and I was keen to go. It seemed to me that North End must have organised the deal though I hadn't signed anything.'

'I made a point of asking the club officials where I stood and it transpired that Hearts wanted me to play a trial within the next fortnight.'

'However, I was at home on the Sunday when the owner of a lemonade factory next door to our house came to say that a man named McCartney was on the telephone asking to talk to me. I didn't know who he was until the voice at the other end of the line explained that he was the manager of Hibs.'

'He wanted me to sign for them but I wasn't the least bit excited. Indeed, I remember feeling he was a bit of a nuisance to disturb my Sunday!'

'McCartney invited me to meet him at the Seaforth Hotel at Arbroath. He was a flamboyant man with tremendous personality who impressed me very much, and said there was a place in Hibs' team against Hearts the following night if I signed. The manager stressed – and it was a vital argument – that both clubs knew what I could do and Hibs didn't need any further trials for a final assessment.'

'I hedged a decision and told him that my father would have to be consulted. The Hibs boss immediately suggested that I should bring my dad along to the game.'

'Within my heart, I had decided to join Hibs because of the trial business. We met the manager in the North British Hotel around tea-time on Monday, April 28 – less than a month before my 17th birthday – and I received a £10 signing-on fee. I felt like a millionaire!'

'It was straight to Tynecastle for the League game with Hearts and I found to my horror that I didn't have my boots. There was an arrangement that one of my Dundee junior colleagues would bring them along and he let me down.'

'I'm sure some of the senior players wondered what kind of youth would turn up without any footwear. However, Hibs gave me a pair and I was very proud to score a hat trick against big Jimmy Dykes in borrowed boots. We won 5-3 despite three goals by Tommy Walker and that was the start of many happy years with Hibs.'

Gordon even recalls that the derby victory lifted the team into fourth place in the League but there was a let-down for the teenager before the end of the season. He played his part in a Summer Cup run that led to a final against Rangers, and was omitted after laying on the goal against Dumbarton in the semi final at Tynecastle.

'That was a sore point,' he related. 'Hibs signed Jimmy Caskie from Everton in the week of the final and he was promised a medal chance as a current internationalist. Hibs played brilliantly to beat Rangers 3-2 but it was a huge disappointment at that time to miss the game.'

There was consolation on the way in September, 1941 when Gordon had two goals in the 8-1 destruction of Rangers at Easter Road. Most people were reluctant to believe the score-line at first but it was true and Bobby Combe was on target four times.

'Bobby had a marvellous game,' declares Smith, 'and the result typified our attitude towards Rangers. Other clubs feared them but we loved to play them — and beat them.'

'Bobby Combe and Jock Weir both made their first appearance for Hibs on the same night as me. Bobby proved to be a terrific club man in numerous positions and wasn't appreciated as he should have been. He was a manager's dream through his versatility and dropped into the half back line once the famous forward line took shape.'

Gordon reeled off 100 goals in the Southern League and was the club's top scorer seven times between 1943 and 1950, a sequence broken only by the dashing Weir.

He continued to live in Montrose for about a year after joining Hibs and was employed in an insurance office. But manager McCartney was anxious to have him on the spot and persuaded him to move to Edinburgh where he worked in Henry Robb's Shipyard.

He found it a joy to play in front of the classy Matt Busby, who was a guest player, and formed a very high opinion of centre half Bobby Baxter and his inside-forward partner, Willie Finnigan. Hibs lifted the League Cup in 1944 by beating Rangers 6-5 on corners and there was his first call for international duty.

The October match at Wembley was significant for Scotland's all-Edinburgh attack comprising Smith, Walker, Milne, Black and Caskie but mighty England won 6-2 to leave the 20-year-old Hibs forward without any startling memories of his London debut.

Gordon won further recognition against Wales and Belgium before the official resumption of the Scottish League and Hibs went close in the Victory Cup competition of 1946 only to lose to Rangers at Hampden in the final.

They returned to the Glasgow ground a year later to meet Aberdeen in the first post-war Scottish Cup final, having disposed of Rangers in a third-round replay when the expertise of Smith provided goals for Willie Ormond and Johnny Cuthbertson.

In the semi final against Motherwell, at Hampden, the tie had to be decided there and then to avoid a replay so it was a matter of playing extra time until somebody scored. Hugh Howie was the matchwinner for Hibs in 142 minutes with a lob that sailed over the head of goalkeeper Johnston.

Comments Gordon: 'I felt sure we were going to beat Aberdeen once Cuthbertson scored in the first minute but we failed to hold onto the goal and lost 2-1. It was to be the story of our lives.'

Hibs were in irresistible form in the following season and two players shared the eight goals one November afternoon as Third Lanark were outclassed at Easter Road. Alex Linwood collected a hat trick and Gordon supplied five from the wing with a dazzling performance that put his name into the record books.

Willie McCartney died tragically after a Scottish Cup win over Albion Rovers at Coatbridge as Hibs were streaking towards the League title in 1948 and Hugh Shaw was appointed manager.

They met Aberdeen in the third round of the Cup at Easter Road and it was the vintage Gordon who steered Hibs to one of their finest ever successes. Willie Ormond was carried off with a broken leg and goalkeeper Jimmy Kerr had to leave the field with a fractured hand.

Hibs seemed doomed with nine men and wing half Sammy Kean in goal. But Smith's inspiration felled the Dons who could have been excused for thinking they were the handicapped side. Gordon went solo through the middle before half time to put Hibs 2-1 in front and the players went off to an incredible ovation.

Jimmy Kerr was told to play in the second half to reduce the odds and he looks back on the epic and says: 'Gordon beat them single-handed. I couldn't have picked up a cigarette end with my broken hand and I sometimes wondered what I was doing on the park. I had gone out to punch a ball and struck Stan Williams on the head. The injury put me out of the game for 18 weeks but it was good to share in Gordon's 4-2 triumph.'

'It was the kind of game you don't forget,' remarked Gordon. 'It saddened me to see Jimmy pick up that injury which, eventually, forced him to quit too soon. He was some 'keeper and almost invincible at his peak. In our first championship, he was beaten only a handful of times at Easter Road.'

Hibs were fancied for the double until one blunder cost them the semi final against Rangers. There is a lot of silly talk these days about what represents a good gate and it was a mammoth crowd of 143,750 that witnessed Rangers' 1-0 victory. Goalkeeper George Farm misjudged a cross and Willie Thornton's head did the damage.

Gordon was an admirer of inside forward Torry Gillick in that Rangers team and would have liked the opportunity to play beside him. Gillick supplied the ammunition for Waddell to use his power and crossing skill to make goals. Comments Smith: 'It was right that Willie Waddell should be preferred to me in the Scotland side around that period. I saw him play his first game for Scotland in a 5-4 win against England at Hampden and he never let them down from then on.'

There was inevitably a hostile, noisy welcome for Gordon whenever he played in Glasgow, notably at Ibrox and Parkhead. He admitted to me that he loved this individual treatment which was, in its way, a compliment to him. Gordon used to play up to those fans and he gave them reason to boo him in November, 1948 in a 4-2 win against Rangers.

He cut past 'Tiger' Shaw close to the bye-line to smash his first goal from a ridiculous angle, beat Bobby Brown from 40 yards with a rocket shot for another and played keepy-uppy in the most impish manner before lobbing the ball to Cuthbertson's feet for a simple goal. Hibs were four up and won handsomely despite the second-half goals from Rangers.

A missionary trip to the South of Scotland to play Nithsdale Wanderers in a friendly at Sanquhar in April, 1949 marked the birth of the finest forward line in modern football history. The combination of Smith, Johnstone, Reilly, Turnbull and Ormond produced eight goals to give warning of what was in store for future opposition. Gordon had one goal though the significance of the fixture meant nothing to him.

Hibs and Hearts played to a record Easter Road gate of 65,850 on January 2. While Hibs had dropped one point in 13 matches, Hearts stretched their unbeaten run to 11 games by winning yet another derby. It was a commonplace event and another mystery to the fans was the manner in which big Tam Mackenzie contained Smith.

Gordon discounted any notion that the left back booted him out of games by revealing: 'Mackenzie never kicked me. He played hard but his tactic was to stick so close to me that I saw little of the ball. Still, I had some good days against him so it wasn't one-sided by any means.'

'Another awkward full back was Sammy Stewart, the little fellow who played with East Fife. He was an astute player who pretended to make the tackle and then held off and there weren't many better defenders in the business.'

Gordon had netted four goals at Falkirk in the previous season, and he delivered another hat trick in a League Cup thriller at Brockville at the start of the '50-51 season. Falkirk were three goals in front on a muddy pitch when Gordon produced a life-line with a goal before half time.

Just after Hibs drew level, Tommy Younger conceded a penalty and the game had to be won over again. But the winger was unstoppable and supplied the winner in the closing minutes for a hard-earned 5-4 result. The section was duly won but Gordon was under treatment for strained ligaments and missed the quarter-final first leg at Aberdeen. The Dons· won 4-1 and the prospects looked bleak.

Jim Souness was expected to continue at outside right on the Wednesday but there was a dramatic pre-match announcement over the loudspeakers that Hibs' number seven would be ... Gordon Smith. It was just the news the fans needed to roar home the team.

Although his thigh was heavily strapped, Gordon's presence was enough and Hibs were 54 ahead on aggregate when Harry Yorston rescued the Dons in bad light in the closing minutes of extra time.

The teams drew 1-1 after two punishing hours in the Ibrox glaur – both teams received a standing ovation – and, 24 hours later at Hampden, two-goal Bobby Johnstone led his club to a 5-1 triumph after a seven-hour slog.

Alas, the final against Motherwell was another day of dismay for Hibs, who couldn't extend their championship consistency to knock-out matches or, at least, to finals.

However, Hibs could master Rangers invariably, and they did it again at Ibrox in regal fashion. It was one of the team's most distinguished displays as they whipped the Light Blues 3-2 in the Scottish Cup, having conceded a goal in the early minutes of each half to Irishman, Billy Simpson. Smith equalised in the first half, Eddie Turnbull in the second half, and Bobby Johnstone grabbed the winner. As Gordon recalls: 'It was a tremendous performance to give Rangers a goal start twice and beat them so handsomely. It was another example of Rangers holding absolutely no fears for us.' There were 102,00 inside the ground and many more outside. In the first 14 post-war League games with the Ibrox side, Hibs lost only two.

Who could stop the champions now? The answer was the old jinx which struck with a vengeance at Tynecastle in the semi final against Motherwell. Luckless Willie Ormond departed to hospital with ruptured ligaments and left back John Ogilvie headed for the same destination with a broken leg. Back to nine men again!

Gordon had a goal disallowed which would have earned a replay but Motherwell clung on to a 32 lead and he recalls the dreadful conditions the tie was played in.

'Hearts had put down peat moss on the pitch and no type of boot could provide a grip. The park was disgraceful, probably the worst I played on in Scotland.'

The *Sunday Mail's* first Player of the Year award in 1951, presented by Bob Kingsley, was cherished by Gordon since he had been placed ahead of the big-name players in the West.

A testimonial game, promised by Willie McCartney, was arranged for September 15, 1952 against Manchester United, the champions of England. The two title winners were in together and a British decider was no more than Gordon deserved.

It was one of football's classic encounters. Eddie Turnbull hit a hat trick, Lawrie Reilly struck twice and there was a goal each for Smith and Willie Ormond. As Gordon puts it: 'That was a real football game, with the accent on aggression. The score was hard on United but we were good winners.' Two days previously, Hibs stuck six past Morton's Jimmy Cowan and they were in rampant form.

Hibs were denied a championship hat trick by Rangers on goal average and an incredible 90 minutes by Celtic goalkeeper Johnny Bonner snatched the Coronation Cup from the dominant Hibs at Hampden. It was during that summer that the Easter Road men went off to Brazil on tour.

Rio de Janeiro took Gordon's fancy. He said: 'I think the Brazilians were then and still are the best in the world and it was fascinating just to stand on the Copacabana beach and watch barefooted kids keep the ball in the air indefinitely with their amazing control. Brazil don't win every game but they are unbeatable for skill.'

He avoided serious injury until December, 1953 when Hibs went on a goal spree against Raith Rovers. Gordon went for a ball with Charlie Drummond, caught the diving goalkeeper on the shoulder and broke the tibia on his right leg.

Perhaps the enforced rest to the next season benefited him, for Gordon returned in good heart and his international career actually blossomed at the age of 30. He had won two caps in seven years, against England and the United States, before his recall against Portugal in May, 1955.

Scotland were about to undertake a tour of Eastern Europe and Gordon reflects happily on what was a splendid trip for him. 'There was a different atmosphere about this squad of players right from the beginning.'

'The 'Old Guard' had been discarded after a terrible performance at Wembley, and the 'cliques' were broken up. For the first time in international football I felt comfortable and, from the composition of the pool, it was clear that there would be a place for me if I was fit. I scored my first goal in a full international in the 2-2 draw with Yugoslavia in Belgrade. Young was injured there and I was appointed to captain the side against Austria in Vienna.'

'That was quite an experience because I almost started a riot, quite unconsciously, in the Prater Stadium. I was brought down heavily by the full back and I always liked to rise immediately so my adversary wouldn't believe he had hurt me. On this occasion, I was slow to move and the Austrian pulled me to my feet. I shouted at him to keep his hands off me and waved a clenched fist at him.'

'There was a roar from the crowd, fans began to run onto the pitch and it was termed a battle in the papers. But I wasn't involved in any fight despite taking a key role. In fact, the police acted swiftly and removed fans from the field.'

'This incident was not allowed to disguise an excellent performance from Scotland and it was a feat to win 4-1 there. Consequently, the players were in high spirits for the game against Hungary at the Nep Stadium though we were tackling what was easily the best team in the world.'

'I had managed a goal in Vienna and was delighted to score the only goal of the first half against Hungary. It was unbelievable. But they were a magnificent team and put three past Tommy Younger in the second half.'

'For me it was a privilege to play against Puskas, Hidegkuti etc, and a tremendous thrill to captain Scotland against them. At last, I felt I had done myself justice in a Scotland jersey.'

Gordon made six appearances during the year and rejoiced at an invitation to Hibs to compete in the inaugural European Cup. It was the brainchild of French journalist, Gabriel Hanot, of *L'Equipe* and clubs throughout the Continent are indebted to him for his foresight.

Hibs were drawn away first to the German champions, Rot Weiss Essen and, having done more travelling abroad than any other Scottish side, approached the game with caution. Within 20 minutes, however, Hibs felt they had the measure of the home men on a wet night and cruised to a 4-0 success. So it wasn't all that vital when Smith, Younger and Reilly were held up in Denmark and unable to play in the return match at Easter Road.

Djurgaardens, from Sweden, had to play their home game at

Firhill with their country in the grip of winter and Hibs dismissed them to earn a semi final tie with Rheims, from France. It's fair to say that the influence of Raymond Kopa, later to move to Real Madrid, and the play of goalkeeper Jacquet and centre half Jonquet beat Hibs, who had Combe at inside right for Johnstone, transferred previously to Manchester City.

Hibs were beaten 2-0 at the Parc des Princes in Paris and lost 1-0 at home while trying to close the gap. Gordon's view is that the European Cup was launched four years too late for Hibs. He thinks: "If there had been a Champions Cup at the start of the 50s, I am convinced Hibs would have won it.'

He had the misfortune to break a smaller bone in his leg in a tackle with Hearts' Dave Mackay later that year and that meant another period of inactivity.

But the master's touch was sought again by Scotland and in May, 1957, Gordon played in three of the four World Cup qualifying ties against Spain (twice) and Switzerland. A Jackie Mudie hat trick flattened the Spaniards in Glasgow and two points in Basle gave Scotland the right to qualify for the finals in Sweden.

It is one of Smith's regrets that he missed competing in a World Cup final and it was injury that ruined any possibility of an appearance in the Scottish Cup final, also in 1958. The truth is he had his leg encased in plaster after his ankle had been shattered in a collision with Airdrie full back, Shanks.

He told Hibs an ankle operation would be necessary but they weren't interested in financing it. Gordon went to surgeon and friend John Bruce, subsequently knighted and to become chairman of Hibs, for expert attention, and underwent two operations for the removal of bone fragments.

Hibs thought he was finished despite his obvious ability to make chances for ace sharpshooter, Joe Baker, and stunned him with a free transfer at the end of the 58-59 season.

Gordon picks up the story: 'I was sick, absolutely shattered that Hibs didn't want me. I tried to put on a brave face but it was hurtful to be released after what I had gone through.'

'Then the next day, early on Sunday morning, I received a telephone call from Willie Waddell offering me a place in the Kilmarnock team. I'll never forget what that call meant to me.'

'Although Kilmarnock were first to show an interest in me, I felt it was too far away and I reluctantly declined the invitation. Dundee and Hearts were the other clubs who felt I could help them and I plumped for Tynecastle.'

'I had become a fanatical Hibs supporter and so I was very apprehensive about the move to my new club.'

'But I needn't have worried. Everyone at Tynecastle made me welcome and the fans were terrific, too.' Gordon was out to prove at 35 that he was no has-been and the best way was to assist Hearts to land two honours. There was a 12,000 gate at Tynecastle for his scoring start against a Dundee Reserve side in which Alan Gilzean was a new face.

They beat Third Lanark to lift the League Cup and Hearts went on to win the championship by four points from Kilmarnock. Who knows whether Gordon made the difference in the championship struggle but he missed only five games and had booked another shot at Europe's top prize.

A close-season tour of America prepared Hearts for what turned out to be an exceptionally stern test against Benfica, the Portuguese champions. I had been sent to Lisbon for a few days to gather material for a six-day series on Benfica and I suspected they were something special since it was more or less the national team in club colours.

Benfica, with the outstanding Pereira in goal, Germano at centre half and Coluna at inside forward, won 2-1 at Tynecastle and killed off Hearts in the early minutes at the Stadio do Luz.

Gordon played in more than 70 games for Hearts and scored 17 goals but, after two seaons, he moved on and Bob Shankly won his man for Dundee this time. The arrangement was that the veteran winger, operating deeper these days, would travel to Dens Park only once each week on a Thursday.

It worked perfectly in his first season as Gordon's unerring crosses set up goals galore for Alan Gilzean and Alan Gousin. Comments Smith: 'Gilzean was my cup of tea for a centre forward. He was exceptional in the air – as good as anyone I had encountered.'

Craig Brown, Scotland's deputy team coach, was a young member of that Dundee team and he declared: 'Gordon was a smashing footballer. He couldn't run then but he would cut inside and pinpoint left-footed passes straight to his target.'

The formula for success was right and Dundee became champions, three points ahead of Rangers. Gordon had completed the most fabulous championship hat trick and the European Cup beckoned again.

He recalls: 'We had a sparkling run in Europe and were beaten by the eventual winners, AC Milan, in the semi final.'

'Dundee won all four home games and lost four away. Our first tie against Cologne was incredible. We won 8-1 at home and yet struggled to qualify in the end. Their 'keeper had been injured in the first game and they played angrily. The Germans hit us with an avalanche and were 4-0 up when they missed a penalty. I believe they could have knocked out Dundee if they had kept cool that night.'

'We scored four at home against Sporting Lisbon and played exceptionally well to get another four against a smart Anderlecht team who had beaten Real Madrid. In Milan, we were level at half time and paid dearly for trying to be adventurous. Dundee lost 5-1.'

When he left Dens, he had a brief alliance with Morton and the Dublin club, Drumcondra, but it was time to rest on those many laurels.

Gordon doesn't attend football matches anymore though he still follows the game avidly through television and newspapers. He told me: 'I detest the amount of passing backwards, defensive football, obstruction, elbowing and pushing which seems to increase each year – but there are still some wonderful footballers.'

'Where I do envy the modern players is in the great improvement in the ball and the wide choice of footwear.'

He sometimes used to wear basketball boots in the old days but they offered little protection.

Anyone who watched the winger with the gazelle-like movements would appreciate his perfect balance and the ability to conquer conditions whether he was required to perform on snow, ice or mud.

It is no secret why Hibs managed to keep Smith and all the other outstanding players. They were paid well, especially in bonuses but Gordon is on the ball in stating that it would have been impossible to keep the 'Famous Five' together in present-day circumstances.

He says: 'Top players can make a fortune by moving, and the wages are unbelievable. I often wondered what it would be like in English football.'

Newcastle United were so anxious to sign him that Hibs were offered a blank cheque but chairman Harry Swan and manager Hugh Shaw were shrewd enough to hold onto the right players.

Given the chance to play his career all over again, I have no doubt that Gordon would sample football in England or abroad. He thought of joining Cannes at one point following his departure from Easter Road, such is his affection for the Riviera town.

He opened the 'Right Wing' roadhouse in the mid-fifties and remained in the trade for almost thirty years.

It was in his early days with Hibs when they repeatedly retreated down the coast that Gordon thought he would like to stay at North Berwick, and that's where he relaxes with his wife Joan and only son Anthony, born in November 1963.

He chose not to follow in his father's famous footsteps but his ear for music may come from Gordon who was fond of collecting Fats Waller records.

Golf was always the second pursuit of Smith in his playing days and, invariably, he scored under 80. Former Hibs players have their own club for Sunday competitions at Longniddry and he keeps his hand in with Lawrie Reilly, Eddie Turnbull and other well known names.

He suffered a sad loss this year, actually, with the death of South African Bobby Locke, the former Open champion. They were introduced at Glenbervie many years ago and the two families became firm friends.

Another of Gordon's interests is cricket spectating and that surprised me. He said: 'There is nothing better than watching a game at Lord's.'

Although he doesn't diet (he dislikes tea and coffee), Gordon is lighter than when he played and his fit, fresh appearance is a tribute to the way he has looked after himself.

In 1978, I was involved in the organisation of Pat Stanton's testimonial match between Hibs and Celtic and thought it would be a great idea to invite Gordon to turn out at half time with other former players. Just to let the youngsters have a glimpse of the maestro.

He pondered over the idea but declined because he felt it would be necessary to prepare properly and that would mean a training schedule. The perfectionist at work again.

So I suggest we were privileged to marvel at his quality for such a long time and, having watched the big names in big matches throughout the world, I haven't seen anyone better.

Some 400 goals in 900 games are irrefutable statistics and Harry Swan summed him up like this: 'Gordon was associated with Hibs' greatest years. An immaculate player who was the leading light in our 'Famous Five.''

Journalist Bob Kingsley said they should re-turf Easter Road on his retirement as it would never be the same again. But I'll leave the last words to Lawrie Reilly, long-time teammate and friend who declared: 'Gordon was a different class. You've only to look at the goals he scored before the five forwards came together to realise his value.'

FULL INTERNATIONAL CAPS

1944		
*Oct.	England	(A) 2-6
1945		
*Nov.	Wales	(H) 2-0
1946		
*Jan.	Belgium	(H) 2-1
Nov.	Ireland	(H) 0-0
1947		
Apr.	England	(A) 1-1
Nov.	Wales	(H) 1-2
1948		
Apr.	Belgium	(H) 2-0
May	Switzerland	(A) 1-2
May	France	(A) 0-3
1952		
Apr.	England	(H) 1-2
Apr.	U.S.A.	(H) 6-0
1955		
May	Portugal	(H) 3-0
May	Yugoslavia	(A) 2-2 (1)
May	Austria	(A) 4-1 (1)
May	Hungary	(A) 1-3 (1)
Oct.	Ireland	(A) 1-2
Nov.	Wales	(H) 2-0
1956		
Apr.	England	(H) 1-1
1957		
May	Spain	(H) 4-2
May	Switzerland	(A) 2-1
May	Spain	(A) 1-4 (1)

The Scotland score is given first in every case.
*Wartime internationals.

Lawrie Reilly

Lawrie Reilly is the most capped player in Hibs' history and the record marksman for the club in championship football. Two distinctions which enable him to stand out at national and domestic levels.

His goalscoring feats made him popular with fans everywhere and he was dubbed 'Last Minute Lawrie' for his knack of saving or winning a game in the dying seconds.

And, although Denis Law and Kenny Dalglish share the honour of scoring most goals for Scotland, their score of 30 leaves them behind the Easter Road centre forward in terms of achievement.

Lawrie scored 22 goals in 38 full internationals for an average of .57 goals per appearance. Law recorded his goals in 55 matches for an average of .54 while Dalglish took more than 100 games at less than one in every three outings.

A dispute with Hibs and a serious bout of pleurisy combined to cut down his Scotland appearances in 1954 or else Lawrie might have set a goals target beyond his successors.

It was cruel luck that the long illness should prevent him from taking part in the World Cup finals in Switzerland though his presence probably wouldn't have made a lot of difference in the seven-goal defeat by Uruguay.

So he was denied a shot at the World Cup just as a Scottish Cup medal eluded him despite the fact that Hibs were the best team in Scotland, arguably in Britain, at the start of the fifties. However, he has his two championship badges and numerous international honours to prove his greatness in the game.

Wembley sticks out as one of his favourite grounds and he claimed five goals there in five appearances as well as countless headlines.

Indeed, Lawrie had a remarkable start to his Scotland career and was on the winning side in his first dozen matches over two and a half years. Quite a run when you consider international results these days but it all came to an end in Vienna where Scotland were licked 4-0 by the Austrians, who had become the first foreign team to win at Hampden just five months earlier.

While that was unlucky 13 for Lawrie, it is worth mentioning that he never went more than four games without a goal for his country.

Gordon Smith in pensive mood on the beach at North Berwick.

Rangers' defenders Sammy Cox and 'Tiger' Shaw in pursuit of the Galloping Gordon.

Gordon with wife Joan and South African Bobby Locke, his golfing idol who died early in 1987.

A broken leg for Gordon meant a break for defenders who didn't have to face him for some months.

An outstanding Hibs team with the 1952 Scottish Championship Trophy. Back row – Jimmy McColl, Bobby Combe, Hugh Howie, John Paterson, Tommy Younger, Hugh Shaw (manager), Jock Govan, Mick Gallagher, Archie Buchanan, Sammy Kean. Front row – Willie Terris, Bobby Johnstone, Gordon Smith, Harry Swan (chairman), Lawrie Reilly, Eddie Turnbull, Willie Ormond, Tom Hartland.

A reunion for the 'Famous Five' in 1971 when a presentation was made to Jimmy McColl before a friendly against Schalke. The line-up reads – Gordon Smith, Bobby Johnstone, Jimmy McColl, Lawrie Reilly, Johnny Halligan (a teammate of McColl's in the 20s), Eddie Turnbull and Willie Ormond.

Lawrie Reilly eludes Motherwell centre half Andy Paton to slide home another goal.

The ever-watchful Lawrie is ready to pounce if Third Lanark goalkeeper Petrie drops the ball and Bobby Johnstone is on hand, too.

Golfing rivals to this day – Lawrie with Eddie Turnbull, showing a natty style in headgear.

Show business personalities, Andy Cameron and Jimmy Logan, had no chance against Lawrie who was so used to being on target in his playing days.

Two recent pictures of Lawrie (top) behind the bar and (below) in front of his pub at Mitchell Street, Leith.

A boyish Tommy Younger just after signing for Hibs.

Tommy seems to be heading the ball clear in this game against Clyde. John Paterson provides cover and ex-Hibs forward Alex Linwood looks on.

Hibs' great post-war attack known as the 'Famous Five' – Gordon Smith, Bobby Johnstone, Lawrie Reilly, Eddie Turnbull and Willie Ormond.

Three big names in Scottish football at Hibs' centenary celebration – Jock Stein, Tommy Younger and Tom Hart.

A Sunday school shot on the golf course taken before Tommy Younger's death. In the group are Jimmy Kerr, Willie MacFarlane, John Paterson, Willie Clark, Gordon Smith, Jimmy Thomson, Lawrie Reilly, Jock Buchanan and Tommy Preston.

Joe Baker – back at Easter Road for the second time in 1971.

Joe displays the caps he won for England – some with Hibs, others with Arsenal.

He was, of course, a one-club man and spent 13 years with Hibs.

He played football on a 'professional' basis from his schooldays at North Merchiston, for his father Johnny who worked on the railway, used to pay him a penny or twopence a goal. That may not seem a lot but it could be highly profitable for the goal-hungry youngster with sweets at sixpence a bag and comics half that price.

North Merchiston won the League and Cup with his assistance but what was to happen once he switched to rugby-playing Boroughmuir? He tried to combine the two codes, though only briefly, and he preferred to stick to his football with Merchiston Boys Club or Murrayfield Athletic.

But Lawrie revealed: 'I represented the school twice at rugby and I've never forgotten the details. We won 8-6 and 12-8 and I scored all the points from the three quarter line. It was enjoyable but it wasn't for me especially as I had one pair of boots and one pair of shorts.'

Edinburgh Thistle were the crack juvenile outfit at this time and Lawrie played his part in cleaning up the various competitions. Harry Reading, who was in charge of the team, doubled as head groundsman at Easter Road and the cream of his players usually filtered through onto Hibs' books. Harry signed Lawrie as an inside-forward but switched him into the centre after a couple of games.

Lawrie always pinpointed a game he played for Thistle whenever anyone brought up superstitions. It was a local cup final against Musselburgh Union on Friday the 13th and Thistle won 4-0 with all the goals scored by the same eager forward!

He began his apprenticeship as a painter with his uncle, Armstrong Sinclair, a Hearts shareholder who operated from Gorgie Road. Now it was quite logical that the Tynecastle club should be keeping an eye on him with his Bryson Road home within earshot of the ground.

And, sure enough, manager Dave McLean invited him to Tynecastle to discuss signing details. Lawrie's dad passed the news hurriedly to Harry Reading and, before you could say 'goal', Hibs boss Willie McCartney was pushing pen and paper into young Reilly's hands. That is how Hibs won that particular derby duel for the 16-year-old matchwinner.

It is no modern phenomenen for players to indulge in weight training, for Lawrie and Thistle colleague Archie Buchanan were sent by Hibs to Charlie Cotter's gymnasium which used to be situated at the top of Leith Street. However, he quickly made his senior debut against Kilmarnock at Rugby Park where Hibs won 4-3. Soon afterwards, Lawrie collected his first senior goal against Queen of the South and he was on his way.

Lawrie looks back on those early days in the mid-forties and says: 'It was much easier then for a youngster to learn the game. I think there were about six players in the Hibs second team with international experience so you were brought along gradually. Nowadays, reserve teams are full of kids with a captain who may still be a teenager.'

It was against the Dumfries club that he also registered his first hat trick in 1947. Alex Linwood and Leslie Johnstone were the regular attack leaders but he had taken the opportunity to put forward his claim.

The passing of Willie McCartney early in 1948 left Hugh Shaw in charge to hail the new champions and that was the year in which Lawrie burst onto the international scene, though he did not qualify for a League badge. He had never played on the wing until joining Hibs when he sometimes deputised for Willie Ormond.

He didn't really like the left wing, being naturally right-footed, and always felt more confident on the other side of the park. However, he was nominated at outside left in the Scottish League team to play the League of Ireland at Ibrox towards the end of September.

Lawrie was at a bus stop on his way to Easter Road for a testimonial match between Hibs and Manchester United for McCartney's widow when a passer-by congratulated him on his first honour. 'It was the first I knew about it,' he remarked, 'and I didn't know whether to dash back to the house to tell my folks or make sure I didn't miss the bus.' United, incidentally, beat Hibs 1-0 with their goalkeeper Jack Crompton in dazzling form.

The records show that Lawrie scored twice in a 5-1 win yet he hands all the credit to Jimmy Mason, the small, highly skilled Third Lanark inside forward. 'Jimmy made it so easy for me that I couldn't fail.' Anyhow, they were kept together for his Scotland starter against Wales at Ninian Park, Cardiff just 24 days later and the Hibs teenager had the satisfaction of knowing teammates Hugh Howie and Davie Shaw were at full back.

Lawrie was at centre forward but his next five full caps were won on the left wing. Wally Barnes, Alf Sherwood, Roy Paul and Roy Burgess were star men in the Welsh defence but they couldn't pin down the elusive Reilly. Two goals by Willie Waddell and Hugh Howie's one and only gave the Scots a convincing victory.

Later in the season, he was thrilled to appear at Wembley and even more excited to put his name on the scoresheet. Scotland won 3-1 and the newspaper reports were full of one man – Morton goalkeeper, Jimmy Cowan.

'Jimmy was unbelievable that day,' says Lawrie, reliving the glory of those 90 minutes. 'He had the game of his life in much the same way that the Celtic goalkeeper Johnny Bonner beat us in the final of the Coronation Cup in 1953. We bombarded shots at him from every angle and he stopped the lot to allow Celtic to beat us 2-0. Just another final that went astray.'

Speaking of finals, Lawrie admitted that he shouldn't have played in the 1950 League Cup decider against Motherwell: 'We were badly hit by injuries. Gordon Smith and I turned out but we weren't fit and Eddie Turnbull simply couldn't play.'

Lawrie was established as the Scotland leader as Hibs streaked towards their second post-war championship in the 1950-51 season. That elusive Scottish Cup triumph was in sight after the memorable dismissal of Rangers in the third round at Ibrox where Hibs were twice behind before winning 3-2.

They were drawn at Airdrie in the quarter finals and, as it happened, Hibs were due at Broomfield on the previous Saturday in a League match. Lawrie has good cause to remember those matches for different reasons.

Only once was he persuaded to take a penalty and he can relate what happened: 'We were well off for penalty takers with Gordon Smith, Willie Ormond and Eddie Turnbull all proficient at the job. Anyway, I had been potting a few in training so they told me to take this one in the League game at Airdrie.'

'I ran up and hit it with everything. The ball struck the crossbar and rebounded far over my head and outside the box. Back it came and the centre half used his hand to clear so we had another penalty. I politely refused the chance to redeem my reputation and Eddie stepped forward to crash the ball against the woodwork again except that it struck the underside of the bar and bounced behind the line.' Hibs still lost 2-1 – one of only four defeats in the championship which was won by 10 points.

It was tough for any visiting side at Broomfield and Hibs knew it would be hard going in the cup-tie. But the bold Lawrie treated a capacity crowd to a brilliant hat trick and, for the only time in his football life, he was carried shoulder high from the field. But the old hoodoo came back to haunt Hibs in their semi final against Motherwell when they were reduced to 10 men by injuries.

Wembley time had come around again and Lawrie was joined in the side by Bobby Johnstone, the football artist from the rugby stronghold of Selkirk. It was my first visit to Wembley with its marvellous atmosphere and I watched from behind the goal where Harold Hassall shot England in front.

But the Easter Road pair nipped a goal apiece with Billy Liddell as Wilf Mannion went off to hospital with a broken jaw.

That was the first of seven successive seasons in which Lawrie netted most League goals for Hibs and he reeled off more than a century in three seasons in all matches. Hibs retained the title and Lawrie chalked up his first hat trick for Scotland in April, 1952 though not in the traditional dark blue jerseys.

On a midweek night against the United States (who had shocked everyone with their World Cup win against England two years previously) Scotland wore Lord Rosebery's colours and won 6-0. While it wasn't the hardest three-timer he had put away, Lawrie was up against a centre half called Colombo who sported heavy gloves that Reilly thought might have been more suited to a boxing ring.

If Lawrie had topped the 50 mark in the previous season, he was almost unstoppable in the autumn of 1952 and his best ever goal came during a spate of 15 in five games. A hat trick against Hearts, four at Motherwell and one against Dundee were followed by four more in the demolition of the League of Ireland and a single in the 2-1 defeat of Rangers at Ibrox.

Many people have asked him about his most satisfying strike and suggested it might have been a header against Falkirk but he has never doubted the quality of a special event at Fir Park and reckons that particular goal guaranteed him a welcome there whenever he returned.

Lawrie takes up the story: 'We were 4-1 up on Motherwell but they pulled back two goals and it was developing into a struggle. Then, I went for a long clearance from Tommy Younger and back-headed the ball round centre half Andy Paton.'

'As I moved on, defenders kept lunging at me and a forward likes nothing better than opponents who rush in to commit themselves. I managed to clear a few tackles and smacked it into the net on what was a terrific day for me. It was much the same kind of goal that Archie Gemmill scored for Scotland against Holland in the 1978 World Cup in Argentina when the whole defence opened up to let him wriggle through.'

His four goals at Parkhead against the Irish brought much joy and yet a tinge of regret, for it was the nearest Hibs had come to supplying the entire Famous Five for a representative game. Eddie Turnbull was the odd man out and that was a shame even if Billy Steel was a gifted inside left.

Comments Lawrie: 'Eddie's inclusion wouldn't have weakened the team in any way and it's a pity we were never selected as a line. The Press used to urge selectors to send out the Rangers defence with our attack and it would have been a useful experiment to play in front of Bobby Brown, George Young, Jock Shaw, Ian McColl, Willie Woodburn and Sammy Cox.'

Hibs were runnners up in the championship but launched an exciting bid for the special Coronation Cup, mentioned earlier for Bonner's heroics. Hibs disposed of Tottenham and Newcastle but fell to an inspired 'keeper before more than 100,000 spectators at Hampden.

Lawrie had refused to re-sign but that did not stop him from going with the club on their tour of Brazil. A hotel on the famous Copacabana beach was one of the features of an engrossing trip. While they lost to Botafogo and Fluminense and drew with Vasco da Gama through two Reilly goals, Hibs had not been afraid to meet the bewildering Brazilians on their own territory.

However, storm clouds were gathering as Lawrie pursued his demands for a testimonial match. Hugh Shaw did not approve of these occasions and indicated that Gordon Smith's match against Manchester United had been promised to him by the late Willie McCartney.

A transfer request was submitted, and to the horror of the Hibs faithful the management agreed to accept offers. Lawrie made it clear that he wasn't interested in England and Stirling Albion tried to pull off a coup with a £17,000 bid. In fact, Arsenal sent former player, Billy Blyth, to discuss a move to Highbury but Reilly told him he had no desire to go.

Lawrie might have landed with Rangers and he explains why: 'I was friendly with Willie Woodburn, George Young and other Ibrox players through mixing with them on international trips. They wanted me to join them but the fact is that Rangers did not make an offer.'

'I took a job outside the game selling paint but, when the season started without me, I was actually better off financially due to the money I was paid by newspapers.'

He was asked to give his views of Hibs' opening League match against Raith Rovers at Stark's Park and watched from behind the goal as his teammates were crushed 4-0. It was a bad day all round because referee Joe Jackson gave Eddie Turnbull his marching orders.

Tommy D'Arcy, a former junior internationalist from Armadale, filled the centre forward vacancy but Hibs had a most unhappy start to the championship and crashed 4-0 to Hearts in their next game, when Bobby Combe wore the number nine jersey.

There were interested parties outwith Easter Road who wanted the internal trouble patched up and a mediator emerged in the form of the SFA secretary, George Graham, who was knighted subsequently.

He didn't like the idea of Scotland having to do without their lively leader and called him through to Glasgow with a proposition that an international select could be put together for his benefit.

Hibs were content and Lawrie returned to the fold at Old Trafford of all places on September 30. And just to prove he hadn't lost his flair, Reilly supplied both goals in a 2-2 draw.

Another double in the League Cup semi final at Tynecastle was not enough to prevent East Fife sweeping through on a 3-2 margin with two goals from full back Don Emery, one of them a typical cannonball from the penalty spot.

Although Scotland had beaten Ireland, a hat trick at Falkirk helped Lawrie to regain his international place against Wales and he marked his comeback with a goal.

But the season which had started unsatisfactorily turned into the unluckiest and shortest of his career and the familiar Easter Road cry of 'Gie the ba' tae Reilly' was muffled for months when illness struck.

He played in a Scottish Cup tie against Aberdeen in February without feeling at his best. Hibs were beaten and what had seemed no worse than a heavy cold developed into pleurisy and pneumonia.

Lawrie was removed to hospital for expert treatment, and even World Cup football was out of his thoughts as he recovered his strength.

A holiday in Denmark was prescribed as the ideal pick-me-up and Lawrie sailed from Leith in a boat skippered by David Sinclair who became a close friend. During the visit, Lawrie discovered a pair of cut-away style football boots with screw-in studs and enthusiastically showed off his new buy which, at that time, cost only a few pounds. Hibs were encouraged to kit out the team rather than simply chop down the usual long studs!

Lawrie had to wait until the season was under way to receive the go-ahead from hospital to resume training. He actually missed the inauguration of Hibs' floodlights against Hearts though there was always the satisfaction of scoring the first goal under the 'lights in a full-scale rehearsal.

He played at Reading in a friendly and set his sights on facing the great Hungarians who were due to appear at Hampden in December. The SFA decided on a trial match at Falkirk and couldn't have selected a worse night for players or spectators.

A gale howled, rain lashed down and the pitch was ankle deep in mud. To describe the conditions as punishing was a major understatement. Lawrie remembers that it was so cold and wet that the players went into the shower at half time with their strips on to warm up.

There was some anxiety whether Lawrie would come through such a gruelling 90 minutes after his illness but he confesses to having enjoyed the 3-3 draw and his determination paid off.

He was in against Hungary, who had outclassed England in a 6-3 win at Wembley, and that was a Hampden occasion not to be missed with the legendary Puskas, Hidegkuti, Bozsik, Kocsis and goalkeeper Grosics. They were the best in the world despite the fact that West Germany had beaten them for the Jules Rimet Trophy.

Scotland battled manfully against superior opponents and lost only 4-2 which was far better than England's result in Budapest soon afterwards when they were slaughtered 7-1.

Lawrie had paid particular attention to the deep-lying style of centre forward Hidegkuti and always hankered to have a shot at it. Towards the end of his football life, Lawrie led Hibs' attack from a deep position and was paid the warmest compliment by Sammy Baird who reckoned it was one of the best displays he had seen.

After that horrendous season, he was back in full cry as a Scotland regular and figured in 13 more internationals in a two-year period from April, 1955. I suppose it was fitting that his last full cap should be won against England though the 2-1 defeat at Wembley was not in keeping with his usual display. He failed to score for the first time in five visits but the score was less shattering than the 7-2 walloping of 1955.

A cyst on his cartilage demanded the attention of surgeon Sir John Bruce in May 1957, and the man who later became chairman of Hibs warned that it would be an intricate and difficult operation.

Two cuts were needed and Sir John suggested to Lawrie that the injury might bother him long after his playing days. He was right, too, for the leg is swollen permanently though not enough to be any handicap on the golf course.

Once he was fit to train, Lawrie set off for a break at Lossiemouth with his wife and infant son, Lawrance. News of his presence in the town spread so quickly that autograph hunters even waited for him to come out of the cinema.

He established an immediate bond with the locals and presented a Boys Club with the jersey he had worn for Scotland against England in 1951 which was one of his treasured souvenirs. In return, 17 months old Lawrance was gifted his first football.

It pleases Lawrie to see so many League teams go north nowadays for pre-season games because he felt the area was being overlooked at that time.

Anyhow, one more season was considered enough by Lawrie, who was now running his public house in Leith, and his final appearance was against Rangers at Easter Road. Some onlookers judged that Willie Telfer had given him a rough time but Lawrie never thought so and said farewell with a goal.

The Scottish Cup final against Clyde followed five days later and he wasn't even at the game due to a bout of tonsilitis. So it would have been an unfit Reilly in action if he had been pressed to play for only the second time in that particular competition.

Lawrie loved those confrontations against Rangers in the vintage days of Hibs at the start of the fifties, especially when he could chaff Willie Woodburn about the bonuses.

They always had time for a spot of banter and the darting, quicksilver centre liked to tell Willie that Hibs were on the usual £100 bonus.

That information bugged the Ibrox centre half since manager Bill Struth refused to pay his Rangers stars more than £20 incentive money – even if it was in a cup final!

Reilly had many admirers in the game with his tenacious, needle-sharp play and Rangers skipper George Young once said: 'He's like a greyhound coming out of the traps.'

Gil Merrick, the Birmingham and England goalkeeper, dubbed him as 'my biggest bogey in football' as he invariably scored against him.

And Alfie Boyd, the classy Dundee wing half of the same era, put it bluntly when he commented: 'Lawrie is the best centre I've ever played against.'

When he reflects on a sparkling era, Lawrie is not sore at missing the 1954 World Cup finals through illness but he was annoyed about the tournament four years earlier when the SFA decided not to compete unless they could go to Brazil as British champions.

'That was a petty decision,' he says, 'but it was a shambles then and not a lot has changed when you examine our displays in World Cup finals.'

Lawrie didn't play in the decisive game in 1950 against England at Hampden. Willie Bauld led the attack and struck the crossbar in a game which England won by a Roy Bentley goal.

He was never suspended or sent off in a period when a player had to be cautioned three times to be banned. Two bookings in a season were not uncommon and he blames a sharp tongue for most of his bother. He once appealed against a booking and the letter arrived too late to be considered by the SFA owing to the heavy Christmas mail.

Lawrie laughs at the 'Last Minute' nickname he was given for those late goals in important games. He considers his first vital last-gasp goal was in his juvenile days with Edinburgh Thistle when his contribution made it 3-1 and ensured there would be no need for a replay.

His late father once went through the carefully kept scrapbook to discover there were 19 occasions on which he had nipped in with a last-minute saver or winner. Lawrie scored around 270 goals in official club and representative matches and many more in friendlies and reserve games.

Lawrie had to wait until December, 1958 for the staging of his long argued testimonial match and he never ever found out why it took so long to promote his benefit.

He had retired earlier in the year and a one-game comeback was ruled out of the question owing to the tax laws governing such a match.

Somebody must have grudged him the income for the weather couldn't have been worse. It rained all day so that the 12-goal feast served up by Hibs and an International Select was enjoyed by only 6000 spectators.

Stanley Matthews had promised to make an appearance but he couldn't make it. His presence might have ensured a better financial reward for a fellow internationalist.

Lawrie has been 'Mine Host' in the Bowlers Rest for more than 30 years and his links with football remain evident as he displays a Hibs' jersey from the Famous Five days.

He swopped jerseys with England centre forward Stan Mortensen,

Ireland centre half Jack Vernon and Wales winger Cliff Jones and those used to adorn the walls with other mementoes.

But there is such a lot about modern-day football that Lawrie dislikes. Although there is always a seat for him in the Directors' Box at Easter Road, Lawrie seldom takes up the offer.

He hates the atmosphere which has forced clubs to have segregation because no barriers were needed to keep fans apart in his day. The football doesn't impress him either and Lawrie feels that players are reluctant to do what comes naturally to become personalities as a result of the demands of coaches.

Lawrie talks with some knowledge for Scotland didn't possess a manager or coach when he was up front and the team put things right themselves.

What he would like to see is more 'tanner ba'' antics in the streets. As a schoolboy, Lawrie never went anywhere without a tennis ball which he knocked against walls and still controlled when it came back awkwardly. He would rather see kids learn the skills in this way then spend their leisure hours in front of a television set.

Of all the grounds that he played on throughout the world, there were three which had a special appeal for him. Number one, not surprisingly, was Wembley with its magic atmosphere and the vast army of Scottish supporters.

'It's a tremendous sight for any Scottish player to walk onto Wembley and see the cheering masses. The place was very special and I loved it,' he declared.

'But I have to say that Ninian Park was not far behind in my estimation. The Welsh singing gets to the players and I used to join in when we lined up. It was always quite a lucky ground for me, anyway, and I liked those trips to Wales.'

Lawrie's third choice is the National Stadium in Lisbon where Celtic became European champions in 1967 by beating Inter Milan.

He always regarded the Wembley turf as perfect but reckoned you wouldn't be able to play anywhere if you couldn't do it on the smooth Portuguese pitch.

His own free hours are taken up on the golf links at Longniddry where he remains one of the keenest competitors. His intense love of the game almost made him a scratch player and he was down to a 1 handicap which has increased to 5.

There is something wrong if he fails to have three games in any week, and even when he and his second wife, Iris, slip away to their

Spanish holiday home at Fuengirola, the area has a wide choice of golf courses.

But you can take it from me that his passion for football hasn't diminished completely. He still observes closely what is happening to Hibs, and the regulars in his pub will confirm that he is an avid follower on the box.

FULL INTERNATIONAL CAPS

1948		
Oct.	Wales	(A) 3-1
1949		
Apr.	England	(A) 3-1 (1)
Apr.	France	(H) 2-0
Oct.	Ireland	(A) 8-2 (1)
Nov.	Wales	(H) 2-0
1950		
Apr.	Switzerland	(H) 3-1
May.	France	(A) 1-0
Oct.	Wales	(A) 3-1 (2)
1951		
Apr.	England	(A) 3-2 (1)
May	Denmark	(H) 3-1 (1)
May	France	(H) 1-0 (1)
May	Belgium	(A) 5-0
May	Austria	(A) 0-4
Oct.	Ireland	(A) 3-0
Nov.	Wales	(H) 0-1
1952		
Apr.	England	(H) 1-2 (1)
Apr.	U.S.A.	(H) 6-0 (3)
May	Denmark	(A) 2-1 (1)
May	Sweden	(A) 1-3
Oct.	Wales	(A) 2-1
Nov.	Ireland	(H) 1-1 (1)
1953		
Apr.	England	(A) 2-2 (2)
May	Sweden	(H) 1-2
Nov.	Wales	(H) 3-3 (1)
1954		
Dec.	Hungary	(H) 2-4
1955		
Apr.	England	(A) 2-7 (1)
May	Portugal	(H) 3-0 (1)
May	Yugoslavia	(A) 2-2 (1)
May	Austria	(A) 4-1 (1)
May	Hungary	(A) 1-3
Oct.	Ireland	(A) 1-2 (1)
Nov.	Wales	(H) 2-0
1956		
Apr.	England	(H) 1-1
May	Austria	(H) 1-1
Oct.	Wales	(A) 2-2 (1)
Nov.	Ireland	(H) 1-0
Nov.	Yugoslavia	(H) 2-0
1957		
Apr.	England	(A) 1-2

The Scotland score is given first in every case

Tommy Younger

Tommy Younger played 24 times in goal for Scotland, captained the team on four occasions including two matches in the 1958 World Cup finals, and became the first international footballer to rise to the position of President of the Scottish Football Association.

Sadly, he died in office just three months short of his 54th birthday, having undergone an operation for open-heart surgery just six months earlier.

The big, blond, cheery figure was known throughout the football world which he travelled extensively on behalf of the SFA and the European Union. Indeed, it was during trips to Mexico and Canada in 1983 that his health began to give cause for concern.

Tommy was always a jovial heavyweight from his late 'teens but there was an immediate warning to cut down on food and cigars. He loved company, loved football and packed a terrific amount of activity and enjoyment into his life.

When he passed away in the early days of 1984, Tommy had been associated with senior football for 36 years.

He was born in April, 1930 and, as a schoolboy at Craiglockhart and Tynecastle, he cherished an ambition to play in front of a record crowd at Hampden. He performed there many times, of course, though his first cup final for Hibs in 1950 turned out to be a most unhappy and forgettable experience.

He followed George Farm, another Hibs goalkeeper who attained international status, to juvenile Hutchison Vale. There, his ability was recognised by selection for Scotland against England in a juvenile match at Lancaster.

The Scots won 3-0 and that was the signal for top clubs on both sides of the border to pursue the Edinburgh youngster.

Arsenal and Everton showed a keen interest in his future but he was more interested in home cooking and signed for Hibs in 1948.

Farm was transferred to Blackpool after Hibs had lost a Scottish Cup semi final to Rangers and Younger was established as first-team goalkeeper at the start of the 1949-50 season.

Tommy was an apprentice joiner, a big lad with a huge appetite and his non-stop eating fascinated his older teammates. It was reported that one night at a cinema, he devoured three apples, three bars of chocolate, an orange, ice cream and a variety of sweets. Just a modest filler until he could have something more substantial.

He had been in the habit of winning trophies in minor football and his first big chance arrived in October, 1950 when Hibs faced Motherwell in the final of the League Cup at Hampden.

Hibs were warm favourites because they had scored six goals at Fir Park a fortnight earlier, come through a marathon quarter final against Aberdeen and lost two of their dozen League games. It seemed unlikely that there could be such a reversal of form on neutral ground.

But Hibs were beaten 3-0 and Tommy sold the last goal with a mis-hit clearance to Watters. He couldn't hold back the tears of disappointment at the end.

Eddie Turnbull was unfit and Hibs missed his tireless foraging while a totally unexpected team selection failed miserably. Willie Ormond, who always revelled in his duels with right back Kilmarnock, was switched to inside left to accommodate winger Jimmy Bradley, from Port Glasgow.

The story goes that Ormond had been outstanding in a midweek practice match at inside forward, the important difference being that it was an eight-a-side game with loads of room in which to make runs.

Anyhow, the change went sour and 'Big Tam' as he was affectionately known wasn't the only sad Hibs player after the final fiasco.

Matches against Motherwell in that season were completely unpredictable. Hibs took four points from the League fixtures but crashed again to their Scottish Cup hoodoo in a semi final at Tynecastle where Motherewell beat nine men by a goal.

In February of the following year, it was National Service time for the goalkeeper and he joined The Royal Scots at Dreghorn to team up with centre half and clubmate George McKenzie in a friendship that lasted until Tommy's death.

His call-up papers had no effect on his career at Easter Road and he continued to turn out as Hibs swept towards their second championship in four years.

Eventually, they won the championship by 10 points and could not be caught after trouncing Clyde 4-0 at Shawfield on a Wednesday night. It was all over with three fixtures to go and that wasn't bad in view of the fact that Hibs had been beaten in two of their first three matches.

A posting to the British Army in Germany in June looked sure to create a goalkeeping problem for Hibs but a scheme was devised to allow him to retain his first-team place.

Tommy did extra duties during the week to earn a weekend pass and travelled from his bases at Munster and Munich, via London, to help Hibs to lift the title again by a four points margin from Rangers.

It was costing £40 every week for his return air ticket and questions were even asked in Parliament about the time off obtained by this soldier-footballer with so many flying hours.

There were some dramatic dashes for him if he was delayed through bad weather and missed a connection. Fog was the main hazard and he missed a couple of games when his flight was grounded for that reason. Another time he had to stay in Germany to play in an Army Cup tie.

Younger was considered to be the best BEA customer though some wags suggested it would be approprite to rename the airline BEF for his benefit . . . Back Every Friday!

On December 20, 1952, the airline company took the unprecedented step of making a presentation to their favourite passenger before Hibs crushed Queen of the South 7-2.

It took the form of a plaque in recognition of 76 round trips, covering 150,000 miles at a total cost of £3000. A lot of money, perhaps, in days when the price of admission to the terracing was the equivalent of 7½ pence but just imagine the financial outlay in modern times.

Even with Tommy McQueen, whose son Gordon was to play at centre half for Scotland, and Jimmy McCracken on hand as standby goalkeepers, Hibs felt it had been a good investment to provide BEA with weekly custom.

And yet one hiccup in the travelling arrangements might have prevented Hibs from securing the championship hat trick which they wanted badly. He failed to make it to Kirkcaldy on January 10 for a game against Raith Rovers which the home side won 4-2.

In the final analysis, Hibs lost the flag to Rangers on goal average, both teams having secured 43 points. The system in that era was to divide the goals for by the goals against. Rangers' average was 2.05 compared to Hibs' 1.82.

Yet if the simpler methods of today had been in operation to subtract goals conceded from goals scored, the title would have gone to Easter Road by ONE goal. On reflection, a draw at Stark's Park on that cold January day would have made all the difference.

This was a photo-finish and no mistake, and Hibs were irked that they had taken three points off their great Ibrox rivals and finished second.

Ironically, Tommy missed games after his demobilisation owing to a broken thumb. However, that had mended and his wedding was behind him when Hibs met Celtic in the final of the Coronation Cup, a one-off tournament between the top four sides in Scotland and England.

That old cup jinx struck again for, despite some brilliant football from the Famous Five, Celtic won 2-0 with goals from Mochan and Walsh.

Nevertheless, Younger's reputation was growing and his elevation to international level seemed inevitable. Jimmy Cowan, Bobby Brown, George Farm, Fred Martin and Willie Fraser had kept goal for Scotland and his chance had to come.

He made his cap debut against Portugal at Hampden in May, 1955 in a team which featured Gordon Smith and Lawrie Reilly and there was a 3-0 win to celebrate. Tommy won six caps in that year, not counting a match against South Africa, and came face to face with the mighty Magyars in Hungary.

Younger fancied himself as a goalscorer, particularly at training sessions, and it was before the previous international against Austria in Vienna that he wanted to impress his Scotland colleagues.

He had often swopped roles in bounce games at Easter Road so his teammates on the tour were not surprised when the goalkeeper announced that he would move to centre forward in a practice match against a local Austrian amateur team.

Not only that, he vowed to score a hat trick and a bet was struck between Gordon Smith, who said he couldn't do it, and Lawrie Reilly, who dismissed the poor opposition. Once the game restarted, Smith refused to pass the ball in Younger's direction and there was no shortage of banter on the park.

But Lawrie, who had gone off to give the goalkeeper his fling, encouraged the other players to lay them on. Tommy duly celebrated three goals and Gordon had to pay up in Austrian schillings!

Younger was not exactly content at Easter Road and he had submitted the odd transfer request without any joy. He had a hankering to sample English football and benefit financially at the same time.

Hibs went off to France on tour in May, 1956 and results were not up to their usual standard. A few days after their return, Tommy was summoned to The Royal Scots Club – where else? – in Edinburgh to discuss a transfer to Liverpool, who were in the English Second Division.

He accepted the terms and the fee of around £9000 was reckoned to be a record though Sunderland had paid much the same for Cowan. Billy Liddell and Jimmy Melia were in the Anfield team whose target was promotion.

So it was Younger, of Liverpool, who played against Wales in his next international at Cardiff, though he could have missed the game due to a golf ball.

The Scots were based at Sonning-on-Thames for the match at Ninian Park and it was common practice for the players to have a game of golf after training.

Tommy was minding his own business in one foursome when a tee shot from Lawrie Reilly cracked him on the ankle despite the anxious cries of 'Fore.'

Fortunately, the sting had gone out of the shot before it made contact and the 'keeper played his part in a 2-2 draw.

Golf was one of his chief relaxations. His handicap was cut to eight at Longniddry where he had the good fortune or otherwise to stand his hand in the bar for a hole in one.

The highlights of his international career were still to come and it's odd that 15 of his appearances were against foreign opponents.

Every top player had his eyes on the World Cup finals in Sweden in 1958 and the Scots had done exceptionally well to eliminate Spain and Switzerland in the qualifying competition.

It was a sequence of events in the build-up period that led to him being handed the captaincy of the side.

George Young, the long-time Scotland skipper and Ibrox legend, had planned to retire in May, 1957 following the match against Spain in Madrid. Unfortunately, an internal row disrupted Young's plans for a colourful farewell and the selectors discarded him before the game.

Tommy Docherty was appointed captain but he lasted only until Wembley where a 4-0 beating from England threw the selectors into utter confusion.

There was no team manager to blame and they came up with a seven-change side to play Hungary in a friendly at Hampden before heading for the finals.

Docherty was dropped and Tommy was named as Scotland's first goalkeeper leader since the days of Jimmy Brownlie before the First

World War. It was a distinction which tickled the big fellow and he did not take the honour lightly even if he was the only man in the side with unbroken service over a period of three years.

Matt Busby had been in charge of Scotland but he had been forced to quit after Manchester United's Munich Disaster and no replacement had been named.

However, Busby was at Blackpool with his United squad gearing up for the FA Cup final against Bolton Wanderers and Tommy made the trip from Liverpool to ask the advice of one of the game's wisest men.

As a result, a considerable amount of planning was done with Eddie Turnbull a thoughtful contributor. He had been a revelation in midfield for Hibs and Bobby Collins was also dropping back.

Tommy once recalled: 'Although a 1-1 draw was a good result, we should have won the game. Our talk-in at Turnberry was well worthwhile and the team moved with a smoothness which had been lacking.'

Jackie Mudie, who had scored a hat trick against Spain in one of the preliminary ties, was the Scots marksman and the team remained intact for the final warm-up against Poland with the 'keeper in charge again. Two goals by Collins won that match so the players were in good heart to face the world.

Scotland met Yugoslavia in the first section match and secured a 1-1 draw while France thrashed Paraguay 7-3 in the other match which Tommy Docherty and Archie Robertson, the Clyde inside forward, had been sent to watch.

Jimmy Murray, the hard-shooting Hearts inside forward who scored the second-half saver against the 'Slavs, recalls the situation in the Scottish camp.

'We were very happy with the point against Yugoslavia because they had hammered England 5-0 in the weeks leading up to the finals. And then Docherty and Robertson returned to tell us that the Paraguayans would be no problem.'

'That's where it went wrong for the South Americans were a bloody good side and I recall a six footer with a hair net who gave us plenty problems.'

'Paraguay beat us 3-2 and Yugoslavia defeated France by the same score to leave us at the bottom of the table. The Doc was kidded non-stop by the players who inferred that it was a good job Paraguay couldn't play.'

'We picked up quite a few injuries and Dawson Walker, the trainer, was kept busy patching up casualties before the France game.'

'Scotland needed two points but we lost 2-1 and missed a penalty. John Hewie hit the woodwork so hard that the rebound carried over the heads of everyone.'

Following 24 consecutive appearances, Younger was dropped after the Paraguay game and his place went to Bill Brown. It was the end of the road in international football but it was worth noting that the South Americans had scored three goals in every match and still failed to qualify while France went on to finish third behind Pele's Brazil and the hosts Sweden.

The Scots journeyed home without a win in the World Cup – a matter that was not rectified until 1974 against Zaire in West Germany.

At club level, Tommy was transferred to Leeds United and it was an Elland Road connection which led to prosperity in business once the boots were put away for all time.

He had a bash at management with Falkirk and spent a period in Toronto as a coach. But he had to earn a living outwith the game and Tommy was one of the first people in this country to see the possibilities in fruit machines.

Initially, he went into partnership with his English colleague until he set up on his own and flooded the East of Scotland with his 'one arm bandits' and pool tables.

The lure of football remained, though, and he was offered the chance to return to his favourite stamping ground at Easter Road in 1970 in the capacity of a director on this occasion.

Bill Harrower, the Edinburgh bookmaker, had bought the controlling interest in Hibs from Harry Swan some seven years earlier. Now it was commonly thought that he would be prepared to sell out.

Tom Hart, a self-made, wealthy builder, had the money, passion and ambition for a takeover and Tommy Younger was the go-between who set up the exchange of shares. Nobody was ever told the cost but it was thought to be about £65,000.

The new boss appointed his own Board, including 'Big Tam', and Eddie Turnbull agreed to become manager at a Gleneagles rendezvous. Sir John Bruce was made chairman to perform any public speaking and a new era began.

Hibs were rebuilt into a streamlined, free-scoring force and won the League Cup in 1972. Away from the playing side, Tommy was appointed onto the SFA Council and soon earned a place on the powerful Selection Committee.

Thus, he became a regular at every international home and away and eased himself up the legislative ladder. The European Union was next to call on his services as a member of the youth committee and in the role of observer at European ties.

His nomination for Vice-Presidency of the SFA was thoroughly deserved after five years on the Executive body, and he ought to have succeeded Willie Harkness as top man in May, 1982.

But the pair agreed it was bad planning to have a change in the major office in the weeks just before the World Cup finals in Spain and settled on the status quo for a further year for the benefit of Scottish football.

I had a long session with Tommy less than a month before his installation as President – the youngest, by the way, to hold the esteemed office – and he spoke proudly of his extensive travels on football business.

From mid-March to the beginning of June, his schedule involved visits to Brussels, London, Gothenburg, Porthcawl, London, Mexico and Canada. Tommy probably didn't appreciate that it was all too much for any individual even if he had sold Youngers Sporting Enterprises to Ladbrokes.

They had given him a handsome six-figure cheque to control his fruit machine empire but retained him as a consultant on a salary that was generous to say the least.

He liked his large whiskies, the Havana cigars and the inevitable Piesporter with his meals. A 'Younger measure' in the boardroom at Easter Road meant that one drink was sufficient. He was equally generous when paying out of his own pocket.

Tom Hart once referred to him as 'a cuddly bear' and that was a fair description of the man with a lively personality and a welcoming smile. He would act as Master of Ceremonies at club dances until the pursestrings had to be tightened because they were lavish affairs, and his impersonation of comedian Chic Murray was part of his routine.

Unfortunately, the presidential post coincided with a downturn in his health and he was denied the time to fulfil (or at least try to fulfil) one of his chief aims to bring the European Championship finals to Scotland.

Tommy felt he had enough friends in UEFA to help him towards his goal and he talked of the eight grounds where the competition could be played – Hampden, Ibrox, Parkhead, Pittodrie, Tannadice, Dens Park, Tynecastle and, naturally, Easter Road.

He told me: 'I want us to make the World Cup finals in South America again. Four in a row would be a terrific achievement for a country the size of Scotland.'

They made it all right, with a struggle, but he was a casualty along the way to the sadness of all who knew him well.

He used to say, too, that Australia and the Far East were among the few places he hadn't visited. The Scots had to go Down Under to qualify for Mexico but, alas, that journey came too late.

He died on January 13, 1984, having been Scotland's leading administrator for only eight months. His first wife, Dorothy, had died before him with a similar complaint. They had three daughters and one son who can reflect with considerable pride on what their father achieved on the field and off it for club and country.

FULL INTERNATIONAL CAPS

1955		
May	Portugal	(H) 3-0
May	Yugoslavia	(A) 2-2
May	Austria	(A) 4-1
May	Hungary	(A) 1-3
Oct.	Ireland	(A) 1-2
Nov.	Wales	(H) 2-0
1956		
Apr.	England	(H) 1-1
May	Austria	(H) 1-1
Oct.	Wales	(A) 2-2
Nov.	Ireland	(H) 1-0
Nov.	Yugoslavia	(H) 2-0
1957		
Apr.	England	(A) 1-2
May	Spain	(H) 4-2
May	Switzerland	(A) 2-1
May	West Germany	(A) 3-1
May	Spain	(A) 1-4
Oct.	Ireland	(A) 1-1
Nov.	Switzerland	(H) 3-2
Nov.	Wales	(H) 1-1
1958		
Apr.	England	(H) 0-4
May	Hungary	(H) 1-1
June	Poland	(A) 2-1
June	Yugoslavia	(A) 1-1
June	Paraguay	(A) 2-3

The Scotland score is given first in every case

Joe Baker

'Explosive' and 'dynamic' are two accurate descriptions of centre forward Joe Baker, who made history as the first player outwith the Football League to play for England and then narrowly cheated death in a horrendous car crash in Italy following his transfer from Hibs to Torino.

He never wanted to play abroad because nothing gave him more joy than playing for Hibs and, when they moved to take him back to Easter Road for a second time towards the end of his career, Joe couldn't believe his luck.

His style was based on Lawrie Reilly and Joe developed into a one-man goal machine with two good feet, great pace and excellent ability in the air – a combination rarely seen in modern football.

Goals were his game from primary school days and some of his feats were in the sensational category such as his four goals against Hearts in the Scottish Cup and five against Third Lanark plus, of course, his goals against foreign opposition.

To this day, however, he laments over the fact that his birthplace made him ineligible to play for Scotland. Although he was chosen twice for the Under 15 schoolboys, there was no parent qualification to allow him to wear the dark blue at senior level.

Just imagine how many caps he might have won for his adopted country at a time when Ian St. John, Davie Herd and Alex Young were in competition for the number nine shirt.

Joe considers he was in a no-win situation when he made the England team. In the south, he was thought of as a Scottish player and, in the north, many regarded him as a Sassenach.

Baker's skills could have made him a millionaire in the '80s but money never bothered him even at his peak. He simply wanted to play and rejoice at scoring goals and his disregard for cash will be borne out in this story.

Joe was born in the Woolton area of Liverpool in July, 1940 because his father, who was serving in the Navy, belonged to Merseyside. But his mother, who had given birth to Gerry – another ex-Hibs forward – in New York, felt unsafe in heavily bombed Liverpool and returned to Motherwell when Joe was six weeks old.

That is how close he came to being born a Scot and Joe will always feel cheated on that score. His first steps to fame were taken at Park Street primary school where, at the age of 12, he put away goals six or seven at a time. In one season, his total was far in excess of the century.

Lanarkshire schoolmasters knew they had a special talent in the St. Joseph's boy, and that was proved in a match against Edinburgh at Tynecastle. Joe rapped in five and there were to be more heroics at that ground in years to come.

His insatiable appetite for the game meant he was playing for his school in the forenoon and Craigneuk Boys Club in the afternoon.

A schoolboy cap was inevitable and the fixture against England took him back to his native city and Everton's home at Goodison Park. He scored both goals in a 2-2 draw, and another goal in an easy win over Wales had the scouts in hot pursuit.

My first sight of Joe was at Easter Road in a match between Hibs Colts and Armadale Thistle, and the manner in which he dispatched four goals had star quality written all over it.

Chelsea were the first club to attract him and he agreed to go to Stamford Bridge at the age of 15. Within a month, Joe was so fed up with life in London that he was released.

Hibs had a scout called Davie Wyper who attached himself to Joe and the friendship blossomed to the benefit of the Easter Road club.

Joe recalls how the scout took him to see Hibs play Rheims in the semi final of the first European Cup. 'I couldn't take my eyes off Raymond Kopa though I wanted Hibs to win. He fascinated me with his ability and Lawrie was on the other side so it was a huge treat for me.'

When Hibs signed him, Joe was with Coltness United but he switched to Armadale Thistle to form what was to become a superb partnership with Johnny MacLeod at both junior and senior levels.

Meanwhile, Wyper had found him a job as an apprentice turner with a wagon-building company and keenly followed the boy's progress as he scored 40 goals for Armadale.

Call-up time for Joe was in the summer of 1957 on a part-time basis and he expected to spend a season in the reserves.

But, in the first month of the season, Joe received a message at work to report to Broomfield Park that night for a midweek fixture against Airdrie in the League Cup. Joe had no idea until the team arrived that he was to stand in for John Fraser.

It wasn't his sweetest experience and that debut game remains fresh in his memory: 'Hibs were beaten 4-1 and I was up against big Doug Baillie. He wasn't quick but he knocked me about and I suppose that was the start of my education.'

Hibs didn't qualify and Joe had to wait two months until October for his next chance which marked the opening of Hearts' floodlights at Tynecastle. He had one of four goals and his first home appearance followed that weekend when he was an immediate hit with two matchwinning goals.

And who should be playing at inside right to him against Queens Park but Lawrie Reilly? In Joe's view, though, his hero ought to have been on the sidelines for his leg was heavily bandaged and he didn't look right.

Hibs had a home friendly arranged against Tottenham Hotspur in the following midweek and Joe captured the headlines in a big way with a smart hat trick. The 17-year-old matchwinner had arrived and no mistake.

His terrific acceleration and non-stop style bothered every defence he faced and another hat trick against St. Mirren in November warned that he was on the rampage.

Hibs were nowhere in a League race, eventually won in a canter by Hearts, but they looked forward to the Scottish Cup with Eddie Turnbull proving a magnificent midfield general and Baker capable of turning any game.

Their campaign began with a replay win against Dundee United at a time when Gordon Smith was in a nursing home for an operation on his ankle. And there was great excitement in Edinburgh with the pairing of Hearts and Hibs at Tynecastle in the third round.

Pundits gave Hibs no chance and forgot about the uncertainty of knock-out football and the opportunism of the teenage terror.

Pre-match predictions seemed to be on target once Hearts whisked into the lead but two goals from Joe gave Hibs the advantage and tremendous encouragement while Lawrie Leslie was doing his bit in goal.

Although the Tynecastle side equalised, Joe scored two more for a great personal triumph in a 4-3 win: 'It was a tremendous performance by the whole team. I was playing against Jimmy Milne and I ran him into the ground by chasing every ball.'

Manager Hugh Shaw had made a surprise selection by using John Grant at inside right for his strength and mobility and that was another factor in the result.

A brilliant solo goal by Joe from the halfway line marked a narrow triumph over Third Lanark and Hibs were pitched against Rangers in the semi final.

After a 2-2 draw, Hibs won the replay 2-1 in controversial circumstances. Referee Bobby Davidson disallowed a 'goal' by Ralph Brand who actually fisted the ball behind goalkeeper Leslie so that an alert referee guaranteed Hibs' path to the final.

And now for an astonishing admission from Joe Baker, the youngster who had done more than most to take Hibs into the final against Clyde.

'I should not have played in that final. I was absolutely overawed by the occasion and I think the place should have gone to Lawrie Reilly. He had retired from the game a few days earlier but would have done better than me, though he wasn't too well during that week.'

'In fact, it was a disaster for Hibs. Early in the game, Andy Aitken was crocked by a tackle from Mike Clinton and, as no substitutes were allowed, we had to battle on with 10 men.'

'Andy had been a vital player for us, especially in the semis because he would run all day and make room for me. I should have scored from a Willie Ormond cross which I chested down and then whacked over the bar. Normally, it would have been in the back of the net but I was so tight and tense.'

'Clyde scored a soft goal to win the trophy though I had the ball in the net – off my hand. A linesman spotted the offence and I wish I had been as lucky as Maradona in the 1986 World Cup.'

'We would have beaten Clyde nine times out of 10 and that was the last chance of a medal for Turnbull and Ormond. I know that manager Hugh Shaw would have been blamed if he had left me out and Hibs had lost but honestly believe the team would have been better off without my jitters. I had a bad game by my own standards.'

Nevertheless, 29 goals from 45 games in his first season was great stuff by Joe who retained his position as number one marksman until his departure to Italy.

A hat trick of headers crushed Aberdeen in a League Cup tie at the start of the following season and three more earned a point off Third Lanark. Towards the end of the year, Hibs were two down to a Celtic team with Billy McNeill at centre half when Baker unleashed his matchwinning talents. Joe hit two goals and pounced for the winner after goalkeeper Dick Beattie had pushed out an effort from Willie Ormond.

Two months earlier, Baker had been introduced to international football via England's Under 23 team. Sam Bolton, one of the FA selectors from Leeds United, had been watching Joe and recommended him.

So Joe won his spurs against Poland at Sheffield with Jimmy Greaves and Bobby Charlton completing the inside trio. but he wasn't over-enamoured about his sudden elevation, as he explains: 'I wasn't pushy and didn't mix much because the players had their own cliques. I'd like to say, though, that Maurice Setters was a big help to me. He made a point of trying to make me feel at home and Walter Winterbottom, the manager, was a very nice man.'

A further appearance against Czechoslovakia signalled that he had done well enough and Joe scored with a header against France at Sunderland in November, 1959 to earn praise from the team boss.

Winterbottom, who had been quoted as saying that Joe was better every time he saw him play, took the young centre aside to say he would be in the squad against Ireland later in the month. Joe wasn't only in the pool – he played and scored at Wembley. He had succeeded Brian Clough and gained five successive caps until Bobby Smith took over.

Joe had played with all members of the 'Famous Five' except Bobby Johnstone and that opportunity arrived with the return of the little inside forward from Manchester City in 1959 after winning an FA Cup badge.

Rather more rounded than in his younger days, Johnstone still possessed the class and his influence helped Joe to find the net more than 50 times in all matches. In League football, he bagged a stunning 42 goals and Hibs actually scored 106 times – four more than champions Hearts.

It was an incredible season punctuated by goal bursts from an attack-minded team. They hit seven against Dunfermline before crushing Airdrie 11-1 at Broomfield seven days later. Tommy Preston outdid Joe that day with four goals to three.

In December, there was another double-figure spree away from home with Partick Thistle on the receiving end and two more goals registered by Baker.

His profitable partnership with Johnstone didn't last long, as 'Nicker' went back to Lancashire to play with Oldham.

His Under 23 days weren't over and in a game against Italy at Newcastle, he infuriated the Latins by bundling their acrobatic goalkeeper over the line and the goal stood to give his side a draw.

Back on the domestic scene, Joe took further revenge on Airdrie with four goals – two of them inside a minute – and he went to town against Third Lanark in December, 1960. The floodlights were on from the start, perhaps to spotlight his five goals in an 8-4 result. He scored one of the fastest hat tricks in history in this one in the space of three minutes.

Hibs were involved in the Fairs Cup for the first time, having had a bye against Lausanne in the first round. They were due to play Barcelona at Easter Road but fog caused a postponement and the clubs agreed to reverse the order of the matches so that Hibs travelled first.

Three days after his destruction of Third Lanark, Joe lined up against the best team in Europe, for Barcelona had become the first team to dismiss Real Madrid from the European Cup.

He had not seen a more impressive stadium than Nou Camp but that didn't stop him from continuing his goal frolics. Hibs went two up and later led 4-2 with a couple from Baker and still the arrogant Spaniards seemed to think they could win when they pleased.

They had underrated Hibs in a game that ended 4-4 and Hugh Shaw went on record to state that Barcelona were fortunate to draw. Obviously, they were confident that star forwards Luis Suarez and Sandor Kocsis would see them through in Scotland.

If ever there was a game to remember, it was the second leg at Easter Road. Although the Hibs players felt confident, bookmakers made them 7-2 outsiders and those odds proved to be generous.

Joe did his day's work as usual and travelled by train from Shotts, still in overalls with a haversack on his back. He tells the tale of a night which began when he arrived at the Caledonian Station.

'It was about quarter to six and there wasn't a taxi in sight. Public transport was mobbed as well so I decided to stroll to the ground. Along Princes Street was fine but down Leith the crowds were gathering and it was difficult to move quickly.'

'Anyway, I didn't arrive in the dressing room until almost seven o'clock and the manager was tearing his hair out. The other lads reckoned it was a great joke at my expense.'

'There were over 40,000 in the ground; I scored first and then Barcelona equalised and went ahead. But we roasted them down the slope in the second half and Tommy Preston made it 6-6 on aggregate to set the stage for a thrilling finish.'

'Twice solid penalty claims became free kicks inside the penalty area until Johnny MacLeod was felled in the box by Garay. This time referee Malka awarded the penalty and the Spaniards went berserk.'

'Police had to restore order and that took some time as the poor German official was assaulted by the Barcelona players. It needed a cool hand to take the penalty after such riotous behaviour and we had an ice-man in Bobby Kinloch who had stood with the ball through all the commotion.'

'It was no problem to Bob to smack the ball past the 'keeper – and that was the signal for further mayhem. Suarez knocked down the referee and the conduct of their team was an absolute disgrace.'

'They knew it was over for them and the referee patrolled the pitch in front of the tunnel to ensure a hasty exit. Even then, the Spaniards tried to kick down the door and the studmarks were left for years as evidence of an amazing night.'

Barcelona's weak temperament had been exposed by the flashing runs of Baker and MacLeod and, though the referee should have been much tougher, you had to have some sympathy for Johannes Malka who had been a stand-in for countryman Gunter Tornieton.

There were apologies from embarrassed officials but Barcelona were fined and, subsequently, paid their own expenses in a goodwill visit to Easter Road.

It was such a famous occasion for Hibs that the team should be recorded: Ronnie Simpson, John Fraser, Joe McClelland, John Baxter, Jim Easton, Sammy Baird, Johnny MacLeod, Tommy Preston, Joe Baker, Bobby Kinloch and Willie Ormond.

Joe scored nine goals against Peebles Rovers in a 15-1 Scottish Cup romp but Hibs went out to Celtic in a replay before two other major issues had to be resolved. It was time for re-signing talks and there were two semi-final ties against Roma.

With the Italian agent, Gigi Peronace, buzzing around, there was loads of speculation about Baker's future, especially as the same agent had taken John Charles to Italy.

Joe was on £12 a week despite his international status and rising fame and it was on the advice of senior colleagues that he sought a rise.

Chairman Harry Swan and manager Hugh Shaw presented him with the re-signing papers when it was his turn and they were shocked that he should refuse and ask for more money.

Having been asked what he wanted, Joe told them an extra five pounds would be satisfactory yet the club bosses said they would need time to consider his request.

'They didn't wait long', recalls Joe. 'For the next day's newspapers carried the story that Hibs could not meet my demands. The articles inferred I was trying to cash in and that wasn't true.'

'I often wonder how things would have developed for me if Hibs had paid me the extra money, because I had no desire to play in

Italy.'

Hibs obviously decided that it was time to cash in and preferred to take what was big money at the time – a fee of £65,000 as it transpired.

Roma arrived in Edinburgh for a Wednesday date in April with a smart little sweeper in Losi and two crack South American forwards in Schiaffino and Lojacono. It was the latter whose ball control and swerving shots – one beat Ronnie Simpson from the touchline – made life awkward in a 2-2 draw but Joe increased his personal stock with another goal.

The second leg was arranged for the following week in the newly built Olympic Stadium but it was almost a secondary consideration as agents from Torino and Roma tripped in and out of the Ritz Hotel.

Fiorentina wanted in, too, and I recall how a reputable English journalist with strong Italian links tried to nobble Baker on the team's arrival at the airport. He didn't recognise Joe and asked Eddie Turnbull to identify the centre forward, which was a bad tactical move.

Turnbull advised the man touting Fiorentina's interest to depart with haste.

Despite these distractions, Hibs were keen to reach the final against either Birmingham or Inter Milan as no British side had experienced success in Europe.

It must be said that they almost made it. Before the game, trainer Turnbull had taken aside Baker and Kinloch and suggested they swop jerseys. 'Let's give it a go,' he said. 'We might just catch them out.'

With two defenders marking Kinloch, Joe had much more freedom than he could have expected and two goals had been whipped home before the Italians realised they had been conned. Hibs led 3-1 in fact but the loss of two late goals resulted in another draw and the necessary play-off.

A toss-up for the venue went Roma's way though Hibs were offered travel for a party of 25 and half the receipts. Chairman Harry Swan stayed on after the match to have a holiday in Ischia so it wasn't all gloom when Hibs stuttered to a 6-0 defeat.

The season in Scotland had ended on April 29 and the decider was fixed for May 27. Hibs had no games, stopped training and tried to regain their sharpness in the week preceding the match.

Hibs were out of shape and the four-goal Manfredini destroyed the Easter Road defence as the Italian fans celebrated by lighting paper torches on the terracing.

It was a sad finale to Joe's first period with Hibs, especially after all the excitement of the previous European ties. He became a Torino player on June 28 and Harry Swan declared: 'English clubs are to blame for opening up this market!'

Denis Law was bought from Manchester City a month later and Torino were convinced that they had secured the best marksmen in British football.

Joe took his cousin Hugo Blair with him for company to guard against another bout of homesickness but it was far from plain sailing. The foreign media tailed them relentlessly in pursuit of Dolce Vita pictures, and club discipline could be unfair depending on results.

A missed chance might mean £10 less in the pay packet whereas a brilliant display could earn a gold medallion. Joe scored eight goals in half a season but the February car crash was a terrible experience for all concerned.

This is his description of the incident: 'The whole team was invited to a supporters' function and the coach was there to keep an eye on us. I suppose we had three glasses of wine each in the course of the evening so, contrary to some reports of the accident, nobody had been drinking to any extent.'

'Denis and I shared a luxury flat and we arrived home just after midnight. I had taken delivery of a very fast, two seater Alfa Romeo which was ordered before Christmas and there had been little chance to try it out in the heavy Turin traffic. Unfortunately, as it happened, Denis suggested we should go for a spin when the streets were quiet – and off we went.'

'The car reacted like a frisky thoroughbred and was hard to hold. We took a half roundabout too quickly and skidded into a statue of Garibaldi. I knew nothing of the fight to save my life during the next fortnight when I was in a coma.'

'My Alfa Romeo was a write-off and so was my face. While Denis emerged with little more than a scratch, my eyes, nose, palate and jawbones were in a bad way and I had five operations as the surgeons set about rebuilding my face.'

'Although my eyes bother me in the coldest weather to this day, they did a great job in patching me up.'

Joe's legs were undamaged, at least, and he made his comeback for Torino on a day when Denis Law scarcely moved out of the centre circle. The coach was furious with him and banned him from the ground for a fortnight. He moped around their private gardens and, without a word of warning, had flown home one day when Joe returned from training.

People are inclined to think Joe made a fortune from his stay in Italy. That isn't the case because he signed a three-year contract which wasn't fulfilled and his average wage was around £80 weekly.

Indeed, it was far more profitable for him to be transferred to Arsenal who actually asked him how much he wanted for wages.

Says Joe: 'I didn't know how to answer manager Billy Wright's question and I muttered that the same as the other players would do me.'

'Billy explained they were all on different contracts and we finally agreed on £150. However, there was more to come and he told me I would be paid £1000 for every 10 goals I scored.'

'Now that was the kind of carrot that appealed to me. I scored 34 goals and reckoned that the extra cash was well earned.'

Of course, Wright knew what Joe was made of as they had clashed in a friendly match at Easter Road where the quicksilver Baker had given the former England captain a rather hard time.

Joe went on to record 94 goals from 114 League games for the Gunners and received a plaque from Highbury in 1983 to acknowledge his membership of their exclusive 100 goal club. He had achieved the 'ton' for Hibs by 1959 and collected a total of 164 goals.

His success with Arsenal gained him re-entry into Alf Ramsay's international team and he increased his cap quota to eight with appearances against Ireland, Spain and Poland in midwinter. As he was on target in two of these matches, he had high expectations of figuring in the World Cup to be hosted by England. Joe was named in the provisional list of 40 but was discarded at the nomination of the final 22. He always claimed that the manager couldn't understand his accent!

He left Arsenal after four contented years during which time Joe had taken a fancy to South Africa's climate following a club tour. Nottingham Forest (for whom he scored twice against Hibs in 1966) was his destination and then the next stop was Sunderland as he gradually edged closer to Scotland. Arsenal had paid Torino £65,000 and it was assessed that his transfers had cost £270,000.

In the early days of 1971, Joe was watched by Hibs chairman Tom Hart, director Tommy Younger and manager Dave Ewing in a game at Roker Park and they all met afterwards to discuss a possible return to Hibs.

'I couldn't believe it,' he told me. 'I would have signed for nothing to play for Hibs again.' St. Mirren were anxious to buy him, too, but it was no contest. Joe had shaken on the deal and duly signed on January 14 in time to face Aberdeen at Easter Road.

Hibs had gone 10 games without a win and the recall of a famous forward rekindled hope among the supporters. Aberdeen, managed by Eddie Turnbull, were challenging Celtic for the title and had won 15 League games in a row. Even more impressive was the record of international goalkeeper Bobby Clark who was unbeaten in more than 12 matches – or for 1093 minutes to be precise when the game started.

Joe was appointed skipper for the day by Dave Ewing and it was a popular move with the fans. Needless to say, Hibs brought both Aberdeen runs to a sudden halt with two goals in four minutes from Pat Stanton and Joe Baker. The reborn hero even had a goal disallowed which Hibs didn't require.

Despite his arrival in the second half of the season, he ended it as the club's top scorer in the championship with eight goals. Just like old times even if his tally was confined to a single figure.

In the close season, Eddie Turnbull left Aberdeen for Hibs and, with that appointment, Baker felt disposed to pack his bags. He claims: 'Eddie was a great player but, as a trainer, he overdid it and players often felt washed out.'

'I was in and out the team and didn't play in the Scottish Cup final which we lost to Celtic. Having featured in a drawn semi final against Rangers, I was dropped for the replay.'

'During a break at Turnberry, I ordered drinks on room service and the manager insisted that I must pay the bill. I asked for a meeting with Tom Hart and that was refused point blank.'

'My days with Hibs were finished and Hal Stewart tried to entice me to Morton with the promise of a gate percentage on good days.'

'Instead, I opted for Raith Rovers and gave Hibs a fright at Easter Road in the first leg of the League Cup. I managed two goals in a 3-2 defeat but they were bound to be more careful in the return at Stark's Park and won 5-2 on aggregate.'

It was retiral time for Joe, who followed in the footsteps of many ex-footballers and became a publican. He spent five years pulling pints and found that the lure of the game still bothered him.

He took charge of junior clubs and had a forgettable spell under Tom Fagan with Albion Rovers. His idea was to serve a kind of apprenticeship, for he had a notion to be a manager – and he really wanted to be the boss of only one club.

Joe applied for the Easter Road post whenever it became vacant but he had been out of the limelight for too long and couldn't obtain an interview. He blamed those years as a publican and, subsequently, in the ice cream business for his lack of favouritism with club directors.

He became very frustrated at the lack of recognition of his talents and declared: 'I wish a big club had given me the chance. I was in the game a long time and know what it is all about. A good boss has to be a psychologist and sometimes a marriage counsellor to back up his football knowledge.'

'There are many aspects of the present-day game that I dislike. When I read of players being offered huge sums to sign contracts, I think why don't they offer them incentives to earn the money like I did with Arsenal.'

'What annoys me about football is the number of one-footed players who are considered good enough for international recognition.'

'I know it was no hindrance to Ferenc Puskas to do everything with his left foot and Willie Ormond used his right foot for standing on. But it staggers me to see the shapes that some stars make to bring the ball round to their good leg.'

'There is only one way to be two footed and that is to practise long and hard. It is a weakness which can be sorted out if the individual is willing.'

He and his wife Sonia have a daughter and son and the family live in Wishaw with Joe employed in the building industry. He returned to Albion Rovers to work alongside Tommy Gemmell in trying to lift their sagging fortunes.

He will talk football all day, any day. Joe would love the chance to turn back the clock and start all over again, provided, of course, that he was born in Scotland!

Look what we've won! Manager Eddie Turnbull holds up the Drybrough Cup in 1972, flanked by skipper Pat Stanton and Alan Gordon.

Pat Stanton teeing up for Bernard Gallacher during a get-together at Easter Road.

Pat on the bench with Derek Rodier, George Stewart, Jim O'Rourke and Tom McNiven.

Willie Hamilton's wife Carol and son Billy display the silver salver presented to Willie in Ottawa during a Hibs' end-of-season tour of North America.

A rare study of Willie with Pat Quinn during a break at a training session.

John Brownlie pictured in the dark blue of Scotland.

A Drybrough Cup celebration in the bath and John has a hand on the trophy.

Who cares about the snow? Track-suited Hibs with their two 1972 trophies. Back row – John Hazel, John Brownlie, Jim Black, Pat Stanton, Jim Herriot, John Blackley, Erich Schaedler. Front row – Tom McNiven, Alex Edwards, Jim O'Rourke, Alan Gordon, Alex Cropley, John Hamilton, Arthur Duncan and Wilson Humphries.

A sad sight for Hibs fans as John Brownlie is carried off during the game against East Fife with a double leg fracture.

Tom McNiven, the man who did so much to restore John to complete fitness and regarded by the players as the best physio in the business.

George and Angela Best arrive at Easter Road for the first time with Tom Hart and wife, Sheila.

George on the ball and taking it past Roddy McDonald, the Celtic centre half in those days.

Peter Cormack, then manager of Partick Thistle, and Pat Stanton stand over Alan Rough as he signs for Hibs.

Where did you get that hat? Alan 'borrows' a cap from a Rangers supporter!

Alan smothers the ball in this Celtic (yes, that's right) attack. Tommy Burns is the Parkhead challenger.

Alan's attractive co-driver is, of course, wife Michelle who used to be a model.

FOR ENGLAND

1959			1965		
Nov.	Ireland	(H) 2-1 (1)	Nov.	Ireland	(H) 2-1 (1)
			Dec.	Spain	(A) 2-0 (1)
1960			Jan.	Poland	(H) 1-1
Apr.	Scotland	(A) 1-1			
May	Yugoslavia	(H) 3-3 (1)			
May	Spain	(A) 0-3			
May	Hungary	(A) 0-2			

England score is given first in every case

Pat Stanton

Pat Stanton is one of the few Hibs players who can boast a full set of medals from Scotland's three big tournaments even if he had to join Celtic to complete the collection.

But whatever he did for the Parkhead club in fewer than 50 matches, Pat made his reputation with Hibs. As a schoolboy, there was only one place fitted his ambitions and that was Easter Road, so it was no more than justice that he had the honour of skippering the side to their League Cup triumph in 1972 and leading them in their Centenary celebrations three years later.

He was called on to captain Scotland three times and there isn't the slightest doubt that his cap quota would have been far greater if Hibs had not persisted in playing him at midfield instead of in the defensive role he favoured.

Pat was so efficient in the sweeper position that former Scotland boss Tommy Docherty claimed: 'He is better than Bobby Moore, England's World Cup captain.'

He has participated in more European ties than any other player in the club's history with some funny experiences interspersed between joy and deep disappointment.

Pat often wondered how he would have fared in England, though it was an offer from America that really tempted him while he was attached to Hibs.

There is a hidden hardness and determination about him as he showed to some extent in his managerial bother with the SFA. But he is one of the game's gentlemen, perhaps too kindly and considerate to have dabbled in management.

On that score, Pat could have been with Manchester United today as Alex Ferguson's right-hand man, for he was the one who chose to end the partnership.

'Yes, it's true,' says Pat, 'that I could have stayed with Alex because we teamed up very well at Aberdeen. Although my wife, Margaret, regards herself as a home bird, she was always quite happy to go where I wanted.'

'But there comes a time in the management business when you have to fulfil the urge to be the number one and, when I left Pittodrie, I hadn't a job lined up.'

There was always the utmost respect between Pat and Jock Stein and their paths crossed frequently through the years. Indeed, it was the 'Big Man' who did his damnedest to steer the Holy Cross Academy schoolboy to Fife rather than Easter Road.

Pat had played for United Crossroads and was with Salvesen Boys Club when Stein invited him to East End Park for a trial. Although it went well enough, Pat was training with Hibs from the age of 14 and Walter Galbraith hadn't an easier signing.

He was farmed out to Bonnyrigg Rose who went to the semi finals of the Scottish Junior Cup. They had a notion to change him into an inside forward, and a steady flow of goals persuaded Hibs to use him there, too, once he was called up.

Born in September, 1944, Pat had turned 19 when his debut chance came at Motherwell in October, 1963 – the first of 399 League matches in which he scored exactly 50 goals. He popped in one that day at Fir Park but it wasn't enough to prevent a 4-3 defeat. Apart from marking the start of his senior career, it was Willie Toner's final appearance for Hibs and the first for full back Billy Simpson.

A new era was dawning for Hibs with the arrival of John Parke, Pat Quinn and Willie Hamilton and with his old school chum, Jim O'Rourke, ready to fill a regular place after playing in a Fairs Cup tie against Utrecht in the previous season at the age of 16 years and 85 days!

Hibs had swept through eight League Cup ties unbeaten and Pat found himself in the semi final against Morton at Ibrox. He confesses to missing a sitter in the first game which was drawn 1-1 and a medal chance went out the window in the replay defeat.

His first foreign trip was to the French Riviera for a quiet friendly in which Hibs beat the local Cannes side 3-2. It might have been a more memorable experience if the visit had coincided with the annual Film Festival.

But things were stirring and Stanton and Stein became part of the same outfit and Jock's first move at Airdrie in April, 1964 was to place Pat in defence. Within a few months, there was a trophy on the sideboard.

The two-leg final of the Summer Cup was held over until the following season due to a typhoid outbreak. Aberdeen won 3-2 at home and Hibs took the return 2-1 when Charlie Cooke saved the Dons with a late goal. Although Aberdeen won the spin of the coin for the right to stage the decider, they were swamped by a brilliant performance by Hibs who could afford the luxury of a missed penalty by Pat and he recalls:

'That was a really good side ... Willie Wilson, John Fraser, John Parke, myself, John McNamee, Jimmy Stevenson, Peter Cormack, Willie Hamilton, Jim Scott, Neil Martin and Eric Stevenson.'

Hibs were on the move under Stein's shrewd guidance and within five days in October, they had beaten Rangers 4-2 at Ibrox and Real Madrid 2-0 in a challenge match at Easter Road.

Says Pat: 'There I was on the same park as Ferenc Puskas with the task of marking him. As it happened, he marked me – permanently on the ankle. He caught me with that famous left boot and the evidence of his ability to look after himself is there to this day. But it was an unforgettable night and Real gave us all a gold watch. Mine still goes.'

A season which promised so much with two more wins over Rangers ended sadly for Hibs. One minute they were in fierce pursuit of the championship and cup double, the next Jock Stein had gone to Celtic.

Pat couldn't understand the timing of the move and commented: 'We finished emptyhanded when both trophies could have been won under Jock's command. I always felt Celtic might have waited to the end of the season.'

Bob Shankly was in charge for the summer tour of Canada and America in which the hardest game was the opener against Nottingham Forest in Vancouver where Hibs won 2-1.

In the second half of 1965, Hibs fought through to the last four in the League Cup again after Peter Cormack's goalkeeping skill had been noted in the first home qualifying game against St. Mirren. Willie Wilson was hurt and played out the game on the right wing while Peter shut out the Saints. Even now, Peter likes a shot between the posts in practice matches and is known as 'Yashin'.

Hibs faced Celtic in the semi at Ibrox and Neil Martin scored twice in a 2-2 draw. A fortnight later, Celtic took the replay 4-0 and referee Bobby Davidson sent off John McNamee. Pat remembers: 'After the big boy was sent off, he walked back onto the pitch and I asked what he was doing. His intention was to have a go at the referee but we managed to push him in the direction of the tunnel.'

Just a week earlier Hibs had returned from Valencia where the Spaniards had reversed a 2-0 defeat in the Fairs Cup. The players waited in the dressing room for news of the toss-up which I witnessed in the room of Swiss referee Gottfried Dienst, who went on to handle the World Cup final at Wembley in 1966. The coin he flipped into the air struck a table, bounced off a chair and nestled against the wall with Dienst scrambling on his knees to retrieve it.

Valencia skipper Roberto, head bandaged, gave a whoop of delight when he won the toss for he knew, like the rest of us, that the tie was over for Hibs. Pat talks of how the fair-haired Guillot was their outstanding performer but, at least, there was the share of a 60,000 gate.

An occasional miss by Joe Davis from the penalty spot caused Hibs to lose a Scottish Cup tie to Hearts at Tynecastle but there was consolation for Pat in his first representative honour in March, 1966 against the English League at Newcastle. The Scots won 3-1 and St. James' Park proved lucky again a year later when he was part of a victorious Under 23 team.

His first full cap against Holland in May, 1966 was in a team drawn entirely from Scottish clubs. Holland, inspired by left winger Piet Keizer, gave them the runaround in a 3-0 defeat. Pat had to wait another three years for his next chance following that setback.

Probably the only occasion that Pat wanted Hibs to lose was during a tournament in the United States and Canada in the summer of 1967. There were a dozen clubs each with an adopted city. Ten teams were from Europe along with Bangu, from Brazil, and Cerro, from Uruguay.

Hibs were the Toronto team but with games to be played in San Francisco, Vancouver, Dallas, Houston, Cleveland and New York, they were hopping from coast to coast in a tiring schedule. But it's right that Pat should pick up the story: 'I suppose it was the trip of a lifetime to spend more than six weeks on the other side of the Atlantic but the lads became fed up. We had no wish to be involved in the play-off games which were to take place in mid-July.'

'So, after taking seven points from a run of five games, we had a chat and decided it would be wiser to slow down. Our next game was away to Stoke City in Cleveland and Hibs didn't mean to win. I reported with blistered feet and Peter Cormack called off with an ankle injury.'

'The only problem was that Stoke weren't interested in winning, either, but Hibs lost 2-0 and there wasn't a sad face in the dressing room. We actually slammed Shamrock Rovers in our second last game and drew 1-1 against Glentoran in a storm in Toronto.'

'Earlier in the tournament, which also involved Aberdeen and Dundee United, we beat Cagliara 2-1 in a game abandoned with seven or eight minutes to play. Peter Cormack was sent off and the

Italians were at their most volatile but Hibs kept the points.'

There was scarcely any break for the players who would normally have been starting to prepare for the season when they arrived back.

Easily the most exciting part of the '67-68 campaign was Hibs' involvement in the Fairs Cup. They established a 3-0 lead over Porto in Edinburgh and a quick penalty in Portugal seemed to lock up the tie. Not at all, for Cormack was ordered off and Porto scored twice in two minutes to put the fans in a frenzy. While Hibs held out for a 4-3 win on aggregate, the final 10 minutes felt like an hour.

So to Naples for a 4-1 defeat on a holiday afternoon. Hibs missed numerous chances as a coloured Brazilian called Cane celebrated a hat trick. However, a second-half goal by Colin Stein gave Hibs huge encouragement for the second leg, especially as Cormack had been suspended for that one game.

Pat reflects: 'It was a false score-line in Italy and we knew they would be vulnerable. But Naples thought they had done enough and didn't bother to bring Altafini with them. With a three-goal lead and Dino Zoff in goal, they were super confident and had no idea how formidable we could be at Easter Road.'

'When the Italians trained on the night before the game, Pesaola, the coach, watched from the Directors' Box with a large whisky in his hand. He needed another one when we were finished with them.'

'Right back Bobby Duncan lashed a long-range left-footer (would you believe) past Zoff to start the goal barrage that was to follow. Pat Quinn scored another before half time and Naples were tottering. We knew during the break that it was only a matter of time with Hibs kicking down their favourite slope.'

'Peter Cormack, Colin Stein and I scored in the one-way traffic so that Hibs had a goal to spare in the 5-0 rout. Four would have done with that away goal. Nobody believed an Italian team could lose by that margin but Hibs had proved anything was possible.'

Don Revie's Leeds United, with their array of big names, awaited Hibs in a Scotland-England confrontation. Hibs appeared to be in trouble at Elland Road once that hard-shooting Scot, Peter Lorimer, put Leeds in front. But United were so hard pressed to stay in front that Colin Stein was subjected to some awful abuse. The Irish referee refused him a blatant penalty and O'Rourke had to replace the injured centre forward.

More than 40,000 fans saw the replay in which Stein, who had missed two games after his Leeds ordeal, had revenge by scoring the first goal. Near the end, Welsh referee Clive Thomas, who loved nothing better than to hog the headlines, gave an indirect free kick against Willie Wilson in the penalty box for taking too many steps. Jack Charlton took up his goal-line stance to head the equaliser and take Leeds through. They went on to win the Fairs Cup and the League Cup as a matter of interest but Hibs' players were annoyed.

Pat explained: 'Gary Sprake, the Leeds goalkeeper, had carried the ball for as many steps as he liked and was never penalised. It was a very unfair decision that cost us the game.'

Stanton broke a big toe at Airdrie and sat out seven of the last eight league fixtures, thus making way for the introduction of John Blackley.

Hibs had another near miss in the League Cup when they were due to play Celtic in the autumn final and the match was delayed until April after the Hampden stand had been damaged by fire.

Despite a few days' preparation at North Berwick, Hibs' hopes went up in smoke rather quickly and Celtic handed out a 6-2 hammering. But that '68-69 season had its moments for Pat.

'I was sent off in a League Cup tie against St. Johnstone at Perth for kicking Bill McGarry. The SFA suspended me for six days and I was fined £30. Colin Stein departed to Rangers and Joe McBride joined us to provide goals in another interesting European campaign.'

'Hibs won both home and away against Olympia, from Yugoslavia, and Lokomotiv Leipzig, from East Germany. Four straight wins was good going and Joe had scored a hat trick against the Germans but now we were heading for Hamburg.'

'Conditions in the Volksparkstadion for the first leg were terrible and any domestic game would have been postponed. But we had flown from Scotland and the referee from Belgium and play went on despite a frosty ground and poor visibility. The fog was bad and you certainly couldn't see both goals at the same time but Hibs played well and came away with a one-goal defeat.'

'You could say we were unfortunate in the second leg. Two goals from Joe McBride counted, three others were disallowed by the Swedish official and Peter Cormack was entitled to be upset at his luck. Joe Davis, an acknowledged expert from the spot, missed a penalty and the Hamburg veteran, Uwe Seeler, slipped away to crack home the goal which counted double with the aggregate level. Another disturbing feature of that game was the fact that Ozcan, Hamburg's Turkish goalkeeper, was allowed to wear a green jersey despite our protests.'

Peter Marinello, who had been dubbed Scotland's answer to George Best, and Peter Cormack were transferred to England following the appointment of Willie MacFarlane as manager. He had been a surprise choice but didn't lack enthusiasm or ideas and was in the mould of Ally MacLeod. In a fairly uneventful season, the introduction of young John Brownlie was a significant step.

In mid-September, 1970, the 48-year-old Tranent builder, Tom Hart, emerged as the new Mr Hibs with 60% of the 2000 shares. He established a new Board which included Sir John Bruce and ex-Hibs goalkeepers, Tommy Younger and Jimmy Kerr. Tom had been wounded in Normandy in 1944 and carried the legacy of a limp which was no hindrance to his ambitions for the club.

Hibs had beaten Malmo 6-0 in the Fairs Cup two days earlier and the new regime were in Sweden for a 3-2 win in which Pat had one of the goals. The Portuguese club, Guimaraes, were edged out and, on the day Hibs were to play Liverpool at Easter Road in the third round, coach Dave Ewing was appointed team boss in place of Willie Macfarlane.

As Pat maintains: 'It wasn't exactly the best time for an upset of that kind. Hibs lost 1-0 and that left us with a mammoth task at Anfield where they beat us by two goals.'

Hibs brought Joe Baker home from Sunderland in time to play in a winning Scottish Cup team against Hearts and Pat recalls the signing of his boyhood idol. 'Joe was my hero as a schoolboy and it was a pleasure to play alongside him though his best days were past. In his manner and everything else, Joe didn't disappoint me.'

'There was a Turnberry preparation for our semi final against Rangers at Hampden and Dave Ewing unexpectedly captured the headlines when he was overheard talking to the team in the dressing room after a goalless draw. He was trying to impress on the players that they had nothing to fear and told them 'Rangers Are Rubbish'. He was astonished to find those words glaring at him from the next morning's newspapers but the damage was done.'

'It was a bit of eavesdropping from behind a slightly open door that did him no favours, particularly as Rangers won the replay 2-1 despite O'Rourke's fifth goal in the competition.'

Ewing's tenancy was brief as he kept the managerial seat warm for Eddie Turnbull, whose appointment was announced in July, 1971. Straight away, he led Hibs to the Scottish Cup final, having made judicious and cheap early buys in Alex Edwards, a football artist with a too-short fuse, and Alan Gordon who had played centre forward for

Hearts and Dundee United with a spell in South Africa sandwiched in between.

Only one goal was conceded – to Rangers in a drawn semi final – as Hibs headed for Hampden with customary high hopes to tackle Celtic. In front of 106,000 spectators, Hibs ran into another six-goal blast like a team in blunder-land. Stanton, permanently in midfield for some time now, looks back on the disaster: 'There was nobody to blame except the players. Our performance was a terrible let-down.'

Hibs were developing into a smooth, scoring machine and hit their peak in the closing months of 1972. In their 11th League Cup tie, they outplayed Rangers in the semi despite the one-goal margin and qualified to meet Celtic on December 9.

This time Hibs were masters from the start and goals from Pat Stanton and Jim O'Rourke had them thinking back in the Eastern Scottish garage that the provisional booking for the open-topped bus would be no false alarm on this occasion.

Celtic pulled one back but not even their noisy choir could knock Hibs off course, and this was the team which received a rapturous Capital welcome for ending a 20-year wait to be among the honours – Jim Herriot, John Brownlie, Erich Schaedler, Pat Stanton, Jim Black, John Blackley, Alex Edwards, Jimmy O'Rourke, Alan Gordon, Alex Cropley and Arthur Duncan.

Says Pat: 'We had a fabulous welcome and it was a great relief to win a cup especially against Celtic. The players were in terrific form at that period. I remember that we scored eight goals against Ayr on the day the Cup was paraded. And then we drew at Celtic Park and beat Aberdeen only 3-2 when we might have scored a dozen goals.'

'We were very confident about the derby game at Tynecastle and it was a dream day for Hibs' fans when we won 7-0 with the cup-winning side. Jim O'Rourke, Alan Gordon and Arthur Duncan had two goals each and Alex Cropley had one. We were on a high until five days later when John Brownlie broke his leg against East Fife.'

His loss was a setback to the team's ambitions in the Cup Winners Cup, in which Sporting had been trounced 6-1 at Easter Road after winning 2-1 in Lisbon. Pat always rated that display as one of Hibs' best in Europe. In their unfamiliar and once-used purple shirts, they stormed the Portuguese goal from the kick off, Arthur Duncan hit the bar, and the winger secured the goal which put his side in a happy position.

Not many people have been to Albania and those who have given it a miss are the lucky ones. Hibs were drawn against FC Besa, whose players ordered steaks for breakfast in the NB hotel and were as bewildered at the way of life as the manner in which they were drubbed 7-1.

So it was a trip into the unknown to fly to Tirana where there were armed guards at the end of the runway. Pat can afford to chuckle now as he recalls: 'We were forced to sit around the airport sipping orange juice for ages and I noticed a guy on duty there who turned out to be a waiter at the hotel as well.'

'Jimmy Kerr had to use all his plumbing knowledge to go around the rooms repairing toilets which wouldn't function. As there was nowhere to go, the management arranged bingo and card sessions to prevent the players from becoming bored.'

Hibs had taken a plentiful supply of food to cater for everyone including the small press corps but the Albanians insisted that we should eat off their menu. Following a verbal battle, the interpreter attached to us to ensure we wouldn't pry too much capitulated and the cuisine improved. At each meal time, Sir John Bruce handed over two bottles of excellent red wine and our genial host produced the local drink which was left untouched.

It was so bad that the journalists were not allowed in the team bus to go training at Durres where the match was to be played. Instead, they sent a rickety old coach specially for us and charged 30 bob each!

As for the game, it is the only time I have spectated from a team's bench, and my request for a telephone which had been greeted with an assurance of 'no problem' really fell on deaf ears. Although my office tried non-stop to make contact during the afternoon. I never heard the telephone ring, possibly because it was stationed in the referee's changing room!

Hibs qualified comfortably with a 1-1 draw and the Italian referee hitched a lift in the club's charter plane to avoid being stuck in Tirana any longer than necessary. A place in the semi beckoned if Hibs could beat Hajduk Split and they should have done. A Gordon hat trick at home earned a 4-2 success though the two goals were avoidable and the Yugoslavs won the return leg 3-0.

After beating Celtic for the second year to retain the pre-season Drybrough Cup, the major event as Hibs chased a title triumph was the signing of Joe Harper from Everton for £120,000 in the following February. Eddie Turnbull considered that his deadly finishing skill would make the difference. But who was to make way for him since Gordon, O'Rourke and Duncan had topped the 100 goals mark between them in the previous season? It was Alan who missed a goalless draw at Falkirk.

Pat has no hesitation in claiming it was bad business for Hibs. 'Harper was a good player and his arrival seemed to strengthen the squad. In effect, his appearance signalled the break-up of a very good side. He was involved in various incidents which affected the morale of the side and was overweight into the bargain. It was another example of a player being signed on reputation rather than current form.'

'I have to say that I didn't like Eddie Turnbull as a person but I respected his knowledge and ability as a manager. He shouted a lot and that did nothing for me and the buying of Harper did nothing for Hibs.'

Hibs were runners-up to Celtic in the championship and there had been the added disappointment of losing to Leeds United for a second time in the UEFA Cup. Tony Higgins passed up two golden chances at Elland Road and there was a repeat of the 0-0 score-line at home – even with 30 minutes' extra time.

'It was a penalty decider and I was told to take the first one,' says Pat. 'The ball rebounded from the post and we were in bother though everyone else (Cropley, Blackley, Bremner and Hazel) scored. It was left to Billy Bremner to make it 5-4 and the ball went in off the underside of the bar.'

'There was no justice in that result and my miss from the spot put me off penalties for the rest of my life.'

Pat led Hibs to another League Cup final in 1974, helped by two section wins against Rangers. But, as always, Celtic stood between them and success and this time the margin was 6-3.

Says Pat: 'Although they had beaten us 5-0 in the League a week earlier, I felt Celtic were starting to lose some of their glitter. We didn't fare all that badly in the final and a little more patience on our part might have produced a better score-line.'

'Celtic also beat us in the Scottish Cup but we managed to master them in the second League game at Easter Road. By that time, Hibs were a new look side. O'Rourke had gone to Motherwell, Cropley to Arsenal and Gordon to Dundee. Ally MacLeod and Roy Barry had joined the club.'

'Before Alex Cropley reluctantly went south, he scored Hibs' 100th goal in Europe against Rosenborg in Trondheim. I even scored twice in the second leg which we won 9-1.'

'But our European days were numbered once we were drawn with

Juventus. Altafini was devastating for them and, though we missed a few chances in Turin, they scored four in each leg.'

Hibs were blown out of the League Cup in a major upset at Montrose in September, 1975, and the events which followed soured Pat's feelings for the club. Having taken a one-goal lead to Links Park and increased it in the first minute through Arthur Duncan, Hibs were in total command. But, in a gale force wind, they lost 3-1 in extra time.

Pat was made the scapegoat and was dropped with Tony Higgins for the home game against St. Johnstone three days later. He rang me to say: 'I'm asking for a transfer. The manager will receive a letter but he knows my view. The whole side had a poor night at Montrose but the fact is I've been playing in a position I don't really like for a number of years. I'm paying for my versatility.'

It was a bombshell for Hibs supporters when I broke the news on the Saturday night, yet everyone felt Pat was bound to be reinstated for the UEFA Cup return with Liverpool at Anfield on the following Wednesday.

Hibs led by a Joe Harper goal, having missed a penalty, and were in with a big chance. Stanton, however, was omitted again and, though Alex Edwards scored first for Hibs, a hat trick of headers by John Toshack put Liverpool through on a 3-2 aggregate.

I can reveal now that Pat was so annoyed by the whole affair that he and John Blackley ignored the midnight curfew imposed on the players after the game and both were fined for returning late to the Prince of Wales Hotel in Southport.

He sat out four games which produced one win and two defeats before being recalled for the fixture at Celtic Park. That was another disappointment because the game was abandoned for fog with seven minutes left when Hibs were two up. One always wonders whether a similar decision would have been taken with the scores reversed.

There were further signs at the start of the next season that the old wounds had not healed for, during a pre-season tour of Eire, Pat didn't figure against the Bohemians and went on as a substitute in Dundalk and Drogheda. What proved to be his last appearance for Hibs was as a replacement for George Stewart in a League Cup tie against St. Johnstone at Easter Road, a game won 9-2.

I had an off-the-record call from Jock Stein on the next Wednesday morning. He asked: 'What chance would I have of getting Pat from Hibs? I don't want to go on and be snubbed.' It was a question I couldn't answer directly but Pat was definitely out of favour.

Well, Jock made the call which enabled Pat to go Parkhead and Jackie McNamara to Hibs. This was the tale of the transfer from Pat's angle.

'I was supposed to play for the reserves at Tynecastle that night and the first team had a home game with Montrose. The telephone rang just as I was leaving the house and my first thought was to let it ring.'

'But I answered the call and Turnbull told me that he had given Stein permission to discuss a move with me. Jock made contact and I gave a speedy "Yes" when he enquired if I would like to join him'.

'My 32nd birthday was less than a fortnight away and here was a chance to move upwards when the message had been coming through that I was on the way out.'

'I don't think for a minute that the transfer was intended to do me a good turn but it worked out that way because I won a Scottish Cup badge and League medal in fewer than 50 games for the club. Jackie went on to do well for Hibs so both sides had reason for satisfaction.'

'My job was to steady the defence. We beat Rangers 1-0 to win the Cup and lifted the Premier League for the first time with nine points to spare from Rangers.'

'But I was sent off for the third time in Australia of all places. It was against the Yugoslav team, Red Star, that I was fouled for no reason and promptly retaliated. Big Jock was displeased to say the least and laid into me for being so silly with all my experience.'

'I looked him straight in the eye and demanded: "What would you have done?" He smiled and turned away.'

A bad knee injury sustained in a tackle with Brian McLaughlin on the training ground at Barrowfield put Pat out of commission for a year. Infection set in following the cartilage operation and he actually lost two stones through that upset.

It was agreed that Hibs and Celtic would play a Testimonial match for Pat and thousands of his new admirers travelled to Easter Road on April, 1978 to pay their tribute. On a drab wet day, more than 20,000 spectators showed their appreciation of an outstanding player.

Although his move West worked out ideally, Pat disclosed that a previous approach in his Hibs days had been very tempting. He explained: 'Like most players, I had a fancy to judge for myself if

English football was all that people made it out to be. Newcastle were supposed to want me but nothing happened and I was too fond of Hibs, anyway.'

'However, Seattle sounded me out about going to America and I liked the idea. So did my wife, Margaret, and the prospect of a warmer climate added to its appeal. I doubt if Hibs would have permitted such a deal but I sometimes regret that it didn't materialise.'

Pat played in 680 games for Hibs and scored 83 goals; represented his country in 16 full internationals, seven Inter League games; three at Under 23 level and once as a senior member of the Under 21s. And he was Scotland's Player of the Year in 1970.

His best year in international football was 1971 in which he won seven caps and played in two winning sides! He says: 'When we met Belgium in Liège on a mud-heap, the place reminded me of Pumpherston with a huge bing at one end of the ground.'

'I scored my only goal in the next match against Portugal in Lisbon – but it was an own goal. Goalkeeper Bobby Clark shouted: "You can always beat me", referring to the goal which ended his long unbeaten run at Easter Road.'

Pat regrets not playing against England at Hampden or Wembley. He led his country against Wales and Ireland in 1973 but was less than 100% fit and pulled out of the London game. 'It was a big disappointment but I couldn't let down the other players,' he remarked.

His last game was in a friendly against West Germany in Frankfurt a few months before the World Cup finals. Of that 2-1 defeat, he claims: 'I was disgusted with some of my teammates who jumped ship. You would have the ball and find there was nobody interested in receiving a pass. It was a shame for Willie Ormond, too. He was underrated as a manager and a very nice person.'

Pat's motivation to become a manager took him to Aberdeen as Alex Ferguson's right-hand man. They were a sound partnership but, after celebrating a League success at Easter Road, he quit Pittodrie. Aberdeen urged him to stay but Pat preferred to seek a job as number one though he had nowhere to go.

Cowdenbeath offered him that chance and, six months later, he moved along the road to Dunfermline. A couple of seasons at East End and Pat was ready to return to Easter Road.

He accepted the offer from chairman Kenny Waugh in the Royal Scot Hotel and succeeded Bertie Auld in September, 1982 with Jim O'Rourke and George Stewart as his assistants. It was no picnic and

Hibs won only one of the first 15 League games, grateful for seven points from drawn games.

Stanton decided that a goalkeeper was needed and bought the best in Alan Rough. 'He kept us in the League', states Pat, who was dissatisfied with the quality of the team he had inherited.

But no money was available to strengthen it and you could sense the frustration building up towards the end of the season. One Friday at the end of April, Pat warned me not to stray too far away from the 'phone, so it was evident a resignation was in the air.

When I went to Motherwell next day and discovered that Pat was not on the team bus, my suspicions were aroused. I had a meeting in one of the Fir Park dug-outs with George Stewart and Jim O'Rourke who didn't want to admit anything but, clearly, knew there were problems.

Before writing a 'Stanton Quits' story, I tried to locate Pat at home or in his pub in the Royal Mile. Actually, he was watching Edinburgh Albion in a public park.

Now Pat fills in the blanks: 'I told Mr. Waugh that it was over for me and that I wouldn't be going to Motherwell. Apparently, he didn't tell the other directors and Kenny McLean learned what was happening from the Pink News. He resigned in sympathy with me, having been vice chairman.'

'Mr. Waugh urged me to think again on the Sunday but it was really my father who was responsible for persuading me to change my mind. So I agreed to carry on though it didn't become any easier.'

'John Blackley became my assistant once George and Jim left and he played in quite a few games to lend valuable experience at the back. Willie Irvine had a great spell in the first half of the season and his goals ensured our safety.'

'But two years to the month after accepting the post, a home defeat by Dumbarton was more than I could stomach and my resignation was accepted.'

'A fortnight earlier, I had been in bother with referee Brian McGinlay and my clashes with the SFA were getting me down. They had doubled a £200 fine which was not paid within their deadline when I had words with referee Bob Valentine. They called it 'indiscreet' but I thought it was a scandalous way to treat any manager.'

'Then my complaint about Graham Harvey being given offside at Pittodrie resulted in another report from McGinlay. My punishment was £400 but, at least, there was no prison sentence!'

'That money was never paid and I have no intention of clearing what I regard as an unjust debt. The SFA won't let me back into football until the slate is wiped clean but that doesn't bother me.'

'I have done some commentating for the BBC and watch Hibs regularly when I can slip away from my Portobello hotel. I also sleep better these days.'

FULL INTERNATIONAL CAPS

1966		
May	Holland	(H) 0-3
1969		
May	Ireland	(H) 1-1
Sep.	Eire	(A) 1-1
Nov.	Austria	(A) 0-2
1970		
Nov.	Denmark	(H) 1-0
1971		
Feb.	Belgium	(A) 0-3
Apr.	Portugal	(A) 0-2
June	Denmark	(A) 0-1
June	Russia	(A) 0-1
Oct.	Portugal	(H) 2-1
Nov.	Belgium	(H) 1-0
Dec.	Holland	(A) 1-2
1972		
May	Wales	(H) 1-0
1973		
May	Wales	(A) 2-0
May	Ireland	(H) 1-2
1974		
May	West Germany	(A) 1-2

The Scotland score is given first in every case

Willie Hamilton

Willie Hamilton was an inside forward of dazzling quality who spent 21 months with Hibs under three different managers and all would have agreed that the slim, fair-haired Airdrie man was his own worst enemy.

Walter Galbraith signed him, Jock Stein nurtured and admired his talent, and Bob Shankly sold Willie to England so that he could sleep more soundly at nights.

Players who knew him intimately marvelled at his skills, sympathised with a health problem and shook their heads at the consistent manner in which he veered off the prescribed routes for any ambitious athlete.

It was a manager as shrewd and popular as Joe Mercer who first appreciated Willie's gift in the colours of Drumpellier Amateurs.

Born in 1938, Hamilton once told me that he never expected to play the game professionally and he left school in his home town of Airdrie to become a bricklayer. The work was useful in toughening him but it wasn't really what he wanted and Mercer persuaded Willie to sign for Sheffield United.

Soon he was on the move to Middlesbrough and, even in those early days, stomach trouble was a constant complaint from the unsettled Scot. After six years in the south, Willie jumped at the opportunity to join Hearts and Tommy Walker concluded a small financial deal with Bob Dennison.

Hamilton had a stunning debut against Dundee in 1962 and scored a goal against a defence that contained several international players.

Before the end of the year, he had helped Hearts to win the League Cup, having teamed up on and off the park with Norrie Davidson, who netted the goal which beat Kilmarnock.

Willie used to drink pints of milk to ease the discomfort from his stomach ulcer but he drank too many other beverages not designed to improve his physical condition. He was something of a nightmare for his manager and trainer and a publicly announced suspension and a cartilage operation hastened his departure from Tynecastle.

But he travelled only as far as Easter Road where Walter Galbraith was on a recruitment drive to avoid the relegation scare of the previous season. Pat Quinn had been bought from Blackpool for

£25,000; full back John Parke from Linfield for £12,000; and now Hamilton for a modest fee all in the space of a month.

Willie made his debut at the beginning of November at Firhill but it wasn't a lucky start because Hibs were beaten by Partick Thistle. He played in most games as the team loitered around the middle of the League table but his career was going nowhere.

Hibs were beaten 5-2 in the first round of the Scottish Cup on a foggy day at Pittodrie and a friendly was arranged at Grimsby a fortnight later when they had a free day.

Willie was forever sick, frequently at training, though it wasn't any physical exertions which made him 'unwell' after the side had been whipped 3-0 at Blundell Park.

John Fraser, a popular figure in Hibs colours as a right winger, centre forward and right back before becoming coach was a big admirer and still chuckles at some of Hamilton's humorous antics.

He recalls: 'The players went out for a drink in the evening and those who had too much clamoured for the bus to be stopped en route to the station. A few of them felt queasy and Willie was seen preparing to be sick at the side of a building.'

'But he was wearing a new pair or suede shoes and didn't intend them to be marked. So he told the lads that he would show them how to protect their shoes and laid a half brick on each foot before emptying his inside. I suppose you could say it was the sign of a real professional!'

While Willie was reputed to be a hard trainer, his trademark was a sweatstained shirt and there were plenty of those once Jock Stein arrived from Dunfermline to take charge of Hibs in April, 1964.

The 'Big Man' was a hard disciplinarian and demanded high standards so he set out to reform Hamilton. One day in the dressing room with all the other players, Stein deliberately tried to humiliate Willie into changing his ways. 'You are a disgrace to yourself,' he bellowed. 'You have been blessed with tremendous ability yet you are ruining a career with drink. Go home and don't come back until I send for you.'

Hamilton was absent for about three weeks, in which time Hibs were involved in the Summer Cup. Hearts withdrew from the competition to play in the United States and Hibs had a play-off with Dunfermline for a place in the semi final. Willie was back for this game and the two-leg semi against Kilmarnock which was won 6-4 on aggregate.

The final against Aberdeen was delayed until the start of the next season owing to an outbreak of typhoid and it went to a third game with the teams level at 4-4. Although Aberdeen won the toss to stage the decider, Hibs gave them a lesson and a 3-1 defeat inspired by the wily, wiggling Willie.

Hamilton and his colleagues may have celebrated with something a little stronger than the 'double coca cola' ordered by big Jock when he sat down with the directors in the Caledonian Hotel.

Before Hibs won that trophy, chairman Bill Harrower had been to Spain to tie up contract details with Real Madrid, five-times European champions, to play at Easter Road in October. It was a bold, enterprising move by Hibs who agreed to give Real a £10,000 guarantee to make the trip.

It was to mark one of the most exciting weeks in the club's history and nobody enjoyed that challenge more than Hamilton.

Hibs upped the ground price to six shillings, the enclosure to 10 shillings, and stand seats cost 24s and 15s for the pleasure of seeing Europe's best. Real insisted that Hibs shouldn't wear anything white so Jock Stein acquired an all-green outfit. The Spaniards wanted to bring the ball and eventually settled for 45 minutes with the Scottish type and 45 minutes with their own variety. Pleas for a foreign referee were dismissed and the SFA appointed Hugh Phillips.

So it was a serious business for Real whose team included the incomparable Puskas, plus Gento, Santamaria and Pachin from the team which had beaten Eintracht Frankfurt 7-3 at Hampden in 1960 in the European final classed as one of the greatest games of all time. Zico and Amancio were other famous names in a squad which contained 15 international players!

Stein's crowd-pulling ways attracted 30,000 spectators to Easter Road to see Hibs become the first team to beat the Madrid masters in Scotland on what was their fourth visit. Peter Cormack, a coltish 18-year-old, left-footed a beauty past Araquistain for the first goal and Zico trailed a Pat Quinn free kick into the net for the second.

That goal, incidentally, was Hibs' 200th against foreign opposition and Real presented each player with a gold watch as a memento of the occasion. Hamilton, of course, had been brilliant and outshone all the household names in the Spanish team.

Three days later, Hibs met Rangers at Ibrox and displayed their startling form all over again to beat the champions 4-2 after being behind twice.

Peter Cormack, who eventually left Hibs for Nottingham Forest and ultimate fame at Liverpool and returned in 1986 as assistant manager, remembers the game vividly and not just because he scored two goals.

Said Peter: 'Willie Hamilton had a confrontation with Jim Baxter before the kick off, both claiming what they would do in the course of the afternoon. Well, Willie beat 'Slim Jim' at his own game, standing on the ball and controlling the pace of the match. I think Willie was probably the only player who could have done that to Baxter.'

'He had a terrific ability and was a great passer. If only he had been handled better earlier in his football life, there is no saying what he might have done. But there was always the ulcer and much of his ill health was self-inflicted.'

Hibs were on the march and lost only to Dunfermline in their next 14 games but it wasn't all plain sailing for the controversial inside forward, slightly balding in his mid-twenties.

It was a few years ago that Stein recalled an incident one Friday morning when Willie shambled in late for training. The manager took him aside, told him he was dropped for the next day and ordered Hamilton to report to Cathkin that night for a reserve game.

Willie argued that he wouldn't be going to Glasgow for any second-team match. But he was there and scored a couple of goals which prompted his boss to instruct him to report to Easter Road next day. Hamilton's reward was reinstatement to the team and he was among the goals again.

A glorious goal from Willie enabled Hibs to win the New Year's Day match at Tynecastle and they were very much in the title chase, just four points behind both Hearts and Kilmarnock with a game in hand. By the end of the month, Hibs had three points less than Hearts but with two games fewer played.

Hibs had beaten Rangers 1-0 at Easter Road in front of 44,000 fans through a Neil Martin goal to register the club's first championship double over the Ibrox men for 62 years. The game was played on a snowbound pitch and Jock Stein had been out with the groundstaff hosing snow off the terracing to look after the needs of the customers.

Unfortunately, the Stein era – short and successful – was drawing to an end, for the call had come for him from Celtic Park. But he had one ace to play with Hamilton's expert aid before his departure to Parkhead.

More than 47,000 spectators crowded into the Hibs ground to see their third-round Scottish Cup tie against Rangers and they witnessed a finale of great drama.

Hamilton and Hynd had scored the goals in a tie that looked set for a replay at Ibrox when Hibs were awarded a free kick with a couple of minutes to go. John Fraser hoisted the ball into the goalmouth, Hamilton went for it and Hibs were through 2-1.

There was a debate in the newspapers about the identity of the matchwinner, not that it mattered to the gleeful manager nor his ecstatic players. John Fraser tells of the dressing-room conversation on the Monday: 'I didn't know if the ball had gone in directly but Willie said he had managed a touch and that was good enough for me. Willie wasn't the type to claim a goal that didn't belong to him though he wasn't sure if his touch had altered the flight of the ball.'

Stein never disguised his feelings for Hamilton as a player even if he had been his sternest critic. He told me: 'Willie had everything. He could match anyone in the game with his speed, stamina, shooting power and two good feet.'

As temporary manager of Scotland in the 1965 World Cup qualifying series, Jock awarded Willie his only cap against Finland in Helsinki. Not a vintage display by the classy forward even if Scotland squeezed through.

Two years earlier, Willie had turned out for the Scottish League in a 2-2 draw with the English League at Hampden, and his previous Inter League appearance was against Italy in Rome in November, 1962.

One of his teammates on that occasion was Rangers' fine centre forward Jimmy Millar, now a Leith publican. He revealed: 'Willie turned up at the airport with his boots and no luggage – and he was dressed in his suit with no coat.'

'The Italians had chosen players of other nationalities like John Charles, Hamrin, Del Sol and Haller but Willie was the best player afield in the first half.'

'It was too bad that he became sick at half time and stayed inside to let John Divers take his place. We lost 4-3 and might have won with Willie in the team for 90 minutes.'

Three representative honours was a meagre haul for a player of Hamilton's renown and Stein's waygoing did him no favours.

Bob Shankly took over as manager. He was from the old school, stood no nonsense, and had enjoyed success with Dundee. Could he keep the momentum going as Hibs sought glory on two fronts?

There were nine games to go in the championship and, though Hibs went to Celtic Park and won 4-2, they lost three and drew one to finish fourth only four points behind Kilmarnock who beat Hearts for the title on goal average.

Much of the spirit and zest had gone out of the side and Dunfermline beat them 2-0 in the semi final of the Cup at Tynecastle to leave Hibs emptyhanded. Exasperated, too, according to John Fraser who had this to say: 'Big Jock's move to Celtic left us poleaxed, a shattered bunch who fell away in the closing weeks. I'm sure Hibs would have won the League or Cup (maybe both) if he had stayed. We had proved ourselves a better side than Celtic even if they beat Hibs in the closing weeks and it was galling that they should collect the Cup under the guidance of the man who had taken us to the semis.'

The season wasn't over for Hibs, however, and they set off on a coast-to-coast tour of Canada and the United States to play nine matches.

Hibs opened in Vancouver against Nottingham Forest which was easily the hardest fixture and resulted in a 2-1 win. Elsewhere, it was goals galore with 15 in Regina, another 11 in Winnipeg and 15 more in Ottawa.

Hamilton had 14 of the 72 goals Hibs put away in nine matches and seven of them were scored in that one game in Ottawa, a feat that earned Willie a beautiful silver salver.

On the morning after the match, Hibs' players were in the bus to move to the airport for a flight to Montreal. One player was missing – Willie Hamilton. As John Fraser was the team skipper, he dashed back to the hotel and found Willie asleep in his room.

John explained what went on: 'Willie dived out of bed, had a quick wash and dressed while I started to put his things together. Although our tour lasted more than three weeks, Willie had only a small hold-all which was soon full. Just as we were leaving, I noticed the salver lying on the table but there was no way it would fit into the small bag.'

'Willie tried it at various angles and I was amazed when he bent it in two and pushed his "trophy" among a few belongings.'

Hamilton preferred to travel light as was discovered on that Scotland trip to Italy, but his treatment of the salver indicated that he wasn't enthralled by his seven-goal display.

Hamilton may have been Shankly's type of footballer but not his type of man and Aston Villa were anxious to lure him back to

England – and to First Division football. They had made an offer on the eve of Hibs' departure to Canada and it was fourth time lucky for manager Dick Taylor.

Willie played in the first League Cup game of the season against Falkirk at Brockville, dropped out for the next fixture with St. Mirren and was transferred for a reported £24,000 a few days later. He played 97 games for Hibs and left many people with happy memories in an all-too-brief stay.

Yet again his stay in the south was short and Willie had a second spell with Hearts in 1968. His itchy feet took him north to play with Ross County in the Highland League but his next step was a longer one.

Willie and his wife wanted to emigrate to Canada with their small son and he went back to bricklaying to convince the authorities that he had a trade.

The Hamiltons settled in Calgary in 1975, but, sadly, Willie died on October 22 of the following year with a seizure of the heart.

Plans for their new life were shattered and his widow left Canada within a couple of months to resettle in Edinburgh, complete with Willie's prized souvenirs from a chequered yet memorable career.

HIS ONLY CAP

1965		
May	Finland	(A) 2-1

Scotland score given first

John Brownlie

John Brownlie would have won a barrowload of caps for Scotland if fate hadn't dealt him a cruel blow at the age of 20 when, already, he had represented his country six times.

Easter Road was hushed on January 6, 1973 when the big right back went down in agony after a clash with East Fife's Ian Printy, a first-season senior from Newtongrange.

There had been an ominous crack as the two players reached for the ball near the halfway line beside the stand and the signal for a stretcher confirmed that the young lion had broken his leg.

Worse than that, the X-rays at Edinburgh Royal Infirmary showed that John had, as he puts it, 'done the fib and tib', and news of that double break was bad for a Hibs team sitting proudly at the top of the league table.

East Fife, managed by Pat Quinn – later to join the club as coach under Bertie Auld – had no intention of being slaughtered by the goal-hungry Hibs and their negative, spoiling tactics turned it into a nasty game.

It was niggly and tough, with Alex Edwards the prime target for the rough stuff in view of his suspect temperament. Referee David Syme booked John Love early on for his treatment of the right winger and Walter Borthwick was cautioned for a similar offence.

East Fife wanted to break Hibs' momentum and they succeeded, so the injury to Brownlie before half time was a major setback because the right-wing triangle of Brownlie, Stanton and Edwards was second to none.

Love continued to abuse Edwards to the extent that Alex threw the ball at the Fife player. The 17,000 spectators were angry when the referee booked the Hibs man for expressing his disgust.

Edwards knew, of course, that it was his fourth caution and that was the quota permitted before intervention by the SFA. As it happened, that particular caution cost him a huge 56 days' suspension because of his previous record. Hibs were without him for eight matches and, happily, the anomalies of the disciplinary system have been improved a good deal since those days.

Brownlie was oblivious to his colleague's misery or the fact that

Alan Gordon's 11th goal in seven games earned Hibs their costliest victory of the season late in the game.

But he looks back now and says: 'I think that match cost us the championship. My injury and the long ban on wee Alex left the team a bit lopsided and affected the rhythm. However, I want to make one point clear and it's that Ian Printy was blameless in the incident with me.'

'The referee did not give a foul and he was correct. I overran the ball, as you would do at some stage in every game, and over-stretched. Just the luck of the game.'

Des Bremner was John's replacement and three points were dropped to the two Dundee teams in the next fortnight. Hibs actually finished 12 points behind Celtic and practically all that ground was lost in the last seven games of the season. Four defeats and three draws saw them finish on a depressing note though there was always the League Cup on the sideboard!

John had undergone an immediate operation to have the bones reset yet his recovery was not straightforward. And, during the summer, it was necessary to break the smaller bone again to ensure that both breaks would heal correctly.

Before he was put back in plaster, John had attended the coaching school at Largs and gained his certificate which cheered him towards his comeback.

John missed 50 first-team matches and, following two reserve appearances, turned out against Dundee in mid-November. While it had been a long haul to regain fitness, the full back reckons he might not have played again but for the influence of physiotherapist Tom McNiven.

'He was an immense help to me with his patience and knowledge,' says John. 'I have the highest regard for him because he knows his profession inside out. That much becomes more evident when you are attached to other clubs and realise his value.'

Brownlie did not re-establish himself on a regular basis immediately but he played in seven of the last nine League games when Hibs produced a spurt to finish runners-up in the championship.

But how did a one-time Airdrie ballboy from Caldercruix come to sign for Hibs in the first place? He could have gone to Broomfield or, perhaps, Aberdeen since the famous talent spotter Bobby Calder invited him to Pittodrie for a trial.

It was a tie-up between two scouts, Gavin Dunn and Dan

Crawford, that led to John playing his juvenile football in Edinburgh with Tynecastle Athletic. Bob Shankly recruited him as a centre half and he played for Edina Hibs while working on the groundstaff. Then he was farmed out to Pumpherston for a year to toughen up in the junior grade.

He made his entry into the first team against Dunfermline at East End Park in the heart of the defence in April, 1970 and actually became a class right back by accident.

Willie Macfarlane was in charge and, when Chris Shevlane was injured in the first League Cup tie against St. Johnstone, John was called off the bench to take up his new position. He made two goals and scarcely looked back even if it took him until near Christmas to be preferred to Shevlane, Mervyn Jones and Bobby Duncan.

His role as a regular coincided with the appointment of Dave Ewing as manager and he pitched John into his first European tie against Liverpool at Easter Road in the 1970 Fairs Cup only hours after accepting the post.

Even before Eddie Turnbull assumed command in the summer of the following year, the brilliant attacking play of Brownlie was earning him a formidable reputation.

Jock Govan had revealed the same spirit of adventure and excellent ball control in the post-war team and John revelled in his overlapping runs which consistently brought goals. And it was in June, 1971 that he gained his first cap against Russia in Moscow.

Scotland boss Bobby Brown was faced with several withdrawals from the squad to play friendly matches in Denmark and Russia and asked Tom McNiven, the 'national trainer, to call in the talented young defender.

John remembers the telephone call as if it was yesterday: 'Tommy wanted to know what I was doing and I told him how I planned to help a builder mate of mine in the close season. He said I could forget that idea, for Bobby Brown wanted me on tour. I had to pinch myself to make sure I wasn't hearing things.'

'It may have been a scratch squad put together at the last minute but it was a great thrill to be included and I thoroughly enjoyed the experience of facing the Russians who only beat us 1-0 when most people anticipated a massacre. Pat Stanton was captain and we played well.'

Scotland had lost 1–0 to the Danes in the first match in Copenhagen as well but the trip was a stepping stone for John and the results weren't bad considering that there were only three players in Russia from the team beaten by England at Wembley less than a month earlier.

This distinction as a teenager marked him as one for the future and Tommy Docherty selected John against Peru at Hampden. He won further recognition in May against England and Ireland and these caps helped to make him forget the Scottish Cup final drubbing from Celtic.

There was a great spell ahead for the Lanarkshire six footer and his Easter Road colleagues. Drybrough Cup wins over Rangers and Celtic and the trophy to show for it and then League Cup glory.

He scored twice at Airdrie of all places in the quarter final and has fond memories of the semi final against Rangers at Hampden where he was the matchwinner. 'I can recall most of my goals for there weren't that many,' he stated. 'I collected the ball about the halfway line, dodged a couple of tackles and a path seemed to open up for me. I thought what the hell, kept going and cracked the ball into the net.'

'It was a terrific feeling to beat Celtic in the final so soon after they had thrashed us. Hibs were in super form at that time.'

After that game, Docherty claimed: 'John Brownlie was the best player on the park. He has tremendous ability for one so young.' Yet it was the same 'Doc' who banned Brownlie from crossing the halfway line in a World Cup qualifying game against Denmark at the Idraetsparken in lovely Copenhagen.

Scotland won 4–1 and John felt those instructions were not so much to curb his attacking flair but to make him conscious of the need for care against the dangerous Danes. Scotland beat the same opponents 2–0 a month later in November and John was very much part of the international set-up.

Brownlie shared in the seven-goal New Year's Day romp against Hearts and it was after the dazzling display that Eddie Turnbull heaped praise on his team. He declared: 'As fine a performance as I can recall in 25 years of playing or watching. Hibs played delightful football at a breathtaking pace and the team I was in did not produce anything like it, especially against Hearts.'

That was Hibs' 14th successive derby without defeat but the run ended months later at Tynecastle where Hearts won 4–1 with John still out of action.

He talks of Alex Edwards being a 'steal' from Dunfermline at around £12,000 but has never deviated in his view that Alex Cropley was the man who mattered in that outstanding team. 'One of the best,' is how he describes the little inside forward who was known as 'Sojer' to his mates after beng born at Aldershot.

Added John: 'Apart from his skill at making chances, he could score goals, too, with that tremendous left foot. He was unlucky with injuries but I was sorry to see him leave Hibs for Arsenal.'

Although Cropley was born in England, he was able to play for Scotland through his father's nationality and much inferior players can boast more than his two caps.

Brownlie's broken leg kept him out of European football for almost two years and a less serious knock forced him to sit out a return tie with Juventus in Turin.

Hibs' team had changed in personnel and John found that much of the tremendous spirit which characterised their best days had gone. He considers the side was broken up too fast and that the new faces for old (like Cropley, Gordon and O'Rourke) did not benefit the club.

In the Spring of 1975, John fell heir to a new job as official penalty taker. Joe Harper, Iain Munro and Tony Higgins had failed from the spot and the takeover materialised in an away match with Ayr.

That initial success was followed by one against Deveronvale in a brief visit to the Highlands and John demonstrated his penalty technique at Cork in a pre-season friendly. In fact, he made a habit of scoring a goal on any tour of Eire.

But he was put to test in the UEFA Cup first-round match against Liverpool at Easter Road. John had popped one in against Ayr on the previous Saturday and thought he would aim for the same spot.

He shakes his head when he recounts the horror of a costly miss: 'I didn't hit it right and Ray Clemence practically bent down and picked the ball off the ground. It was the only penalty I messed up in the whole season.'

Hibs won by a Harper goal and might have knocked out Liverpool if John had scored from the spot since Alex Edwards was on target in the first half of the return match at Anfield.

Gradually, Liverpool clawed back into the game and John Toshack finished the hero when his devastating headwork earned him a hat trick. John blamed himself for Hibs' exit from the competition, and he had his name taken at Liverpool to complete his misery.

At least, the clanger didn't deter him from taking more penalties, and a contribution in Dublin was backed up by a double in the 9–2 demolition of St. Johnstone and one against little-known Oesters in the UEFA Cup. Sadly, the 2–0 margin from Easter Road was insufficient in Vaxjo where Hibs collapsed to a 4–1 defeat. That was bad but along came Arbroath to beat them 2-1 in a Scottish Cup replay – and at home, too!

Hibs were on the wane as four wins from 15 League games indicated after the summer of 1977. Queen of South eliminated Hibs in the first round of the League Cup on a home and away basis and Partick Thistle ended the club's modest Scottish Cup ambitions in a replay at Firhill.

An end of the season tour of Canada was to be John's farewell to Hibs and, appropriately, he scored twice in the last of seven matches in the seven-goal rout of Ottawa Tigers. Ally MacLeod had 16 of the 36 goals scored.

John Blackley had gone to Newcastle in the previous season and that was to be John's destination after a breakdown in the part-exchange deal in which ex-Hearts inside forward Ralph Callachan was to join Hibs.

Chairman Tom Hart was amazed when Callachan didn't sign in the first place and he asked me to speak to Ralph and clarify the terms and his signing-on fee.

Callachan expressed a willingness to sign and the result was a high-speed dash in a Rolls Royce by Tommy Younger and Eddie Turnbull on the morning of August 19 so that Ralph could turn out against Rangers later in the day. They had no time to dally with the papers to be registered in Glasgow. John sat in the stand as the teams fought out a goalless draw.

Anyhow, John was happy to move to Tyneside with Hibs receiving a cash surplus, though his financial settlement from the transfer didn't give his bank balance much of a lift.

He says : 'If I had known then what I know now, my part in the transfer wouldn't have gone so smoothly. I gave Hibs nine years and emerged with a modest cut. I should have held them to ransom, particularly when I think of the testimonial games that have been played.'

'Fortunately, I was much wiser once the time came to leave Newcastle for Middlesbrough four years later and that was a lucrative move for me.'

Bronwlie had a lot of time for Tom Hart but felt that Eddie Turnbull, obviously a good manager tactically, ruled by fear and was detached from his team. Wilson Humphries acted as the buffer between players and boss for a spell and he was a popular member of the backroom team.

John's departure from Hibs after 341 games and 32 goals denied him the chance of a Scottish Cup final appearance at the end of the season. But he was at Hampden for two of the three games to lend his support.

In his opinion, it was 'a total liberty' that Hibs were denied a penalty in the first game when Colin Campbell was toppled in the box by Rangers goalkeeper Peter McCloy. There are a great many spectators who saw the incident and share the same viewpoint. Eventually, a luckless own goal by Arthur Duncan enabled Rangers to win the Cup after 330 minutes of tireless toil.

Meanwhile, John embarked on a personal tour of the north-east and switched from Ayresome Park to Hartlepool before re-crossing the Border for a six-month sojourn with Berwick Rangers.

Last season, John turned out for Blyth Spartans under the guidance of Jim Pearson, the former St. Johnstone forward.

In the future, he wouldn't mind the chance to go into coaching or management and there is time on the side of the amiable defender, still only in his mid-thirties.

John confesses that he used to become angry at losing a goal and that's why he twice received his marching orders – once against St. Mirren reserves and again in a Newcastle match with Blackburn.

But he's a placid individual who cringes only at the mention of David Wagstaffe, the Wolves winger who gave him the worst 90 minutes of his career in an Inter-League match at Middlesbrough.

'We only lost 3–2 but he beat me in every conceivable way and I was never more glad to get inside at the finish', he comments.

If that representative game irked him, his seventh and last cap against Rumania in 1975 thrilled him, and he tells why: 'When Willie Ormond picked me for that match, he confirmed my personal assessment that my play was just as good as it had been before the leg break.'

'I realise that others felt I had lost something but I made a complete recovery and worked extremely hard at Newcastle to prove that to my new club and to myself.'

'I enjoyed playing at the top and, especially, in an attractive vein. You find that forwards don't like being taken on by a defender who has a little ball control.'

Now John is carving out a career in insurance on Tyneside, continuing to live in Morpeth with his wife and two sons, Paul and David, who have displayed a keenness for the game.

Another one of his class would find a welcome mat at Easter Road.

SEVEN FULL CAPS

1971		
June	Russia	(A) 0-1
1972		
Apr.	Peru	(H) 2-0
May	Ireland	(H) 2-0
May	England	(H) 0-1
Oct.	Denmark	(A) 4-1
Nov.	Denmark	(H) 2-0
1975		
Dec.	Rumania	(H) 1-1

The Scotland score is given first in every case

George Best

George Best was a Hibs player for only 325 days from the Friday afternoon in November, 1979 when he signed in London to his final appearance as skipper of a winning team against Falkirk in the following October.

But nobody made a bigger impact in Scottish football during that period than the ageing Irish maestro. If he was unable to prevent the club from suffering the stigma of relegation for the first time in almost 50 years, he deflected attention away from their sorry plight.

It was an imaginative move by the club to follow up my suggestion that Best might help them. On a Monday morning, after a weekend television show in which George offered himself to any First Division club in England, I put the thought to Hibs manager, Eddie Turnbull.

'Not a bad idea,' he said. 'Have you mentioned it to the Chairman?' I hadn't but Tom Hart was quick to respond to any notion which might benefit his beloved Hibs.

'Find out where he is and we'll talk to him', croaked the Chairman – and the Best bandwagon had started to roll with countless headlines to come.

Best had just arrived back from America and was staying with his in-laws at Southend. Within two days, Hibs had received permission from Fulham to talk to him because they still held his registration.

There were those who scoffed at Hibs' interest in Best and reckoned it was no more than a publicity gimmick. But Hibs were deadly serious and attitudes changed sharply when George acted on a call that had been recorded on an answering machine.

He contacted Tom Hart on the morning of Saturday, November 10 to say that he and his wife Angela would fly to Edinburgh for a chat and take in the home game against Kilmarnock.

The Chairman met them at the airport, took them for lunch and escorted the Bests into Easter Road just before the game. Little more than 5000 fans gave him a great welcome when he took his seat in the Directors' Box and again at half-time as he drew the winners in a lottery draw.

Hibs wanted him for 12 to 16 games and Best was impressed by the genuine tone of Tom Hart, a straight-shooter who never hesitated to come to the point. But George hadn't played for five months and needed to lose some weight in a hurry.

So the two parties agreed on a second rendezvous at Ipswich on the following Tuesday when Best was to play in Bobby Robson's Testimonial match.

Messrs Hart and Turnbull booked their flights to London and I had no intention of asking the *Evening News* to send me until the Chairman telephoned to tell me their flight times. 'Surely, you should be there,' he declared. 'After all it was your story and you might as well see it through.'

So I joined them on the flight to Heathrow where a chauffeur waited by a limousine to whisk us to Ipswich. Unfortunately, the traffic was heavy and we barely had time for a meal before the game.

It was evident that the 23,000 crowd had been boosted by the presence of Best judging from the reception given to each player. George and Ricardo Villa, the Argentinian star with Tottenham, were the outstanding performers as Ipswich drew 2-2 with an England XI.

Best was 33 and declared himself only 70% fit. He told three television interviewers that he was considering offers but gave nobody any hint of his intentions. He had promised to talk to the Hibs people in the morning.

We stayed in the plush Carlton Tower Hotel in London, a customary haunt for wealthy Arabs who didn't blink at the extortionate charges.

It was agreed that Turnbull and I should go to the Chairman's suite in the morning after breakfast. When we knocked on the door, he was in singlet and slacks, scanning his diary for Best's telephone number.

You can imagine his shock when there was no reply from the number he tried. However, on re-checking his book, the former builder realised he had been ringing George's agent.

At that point, there was an incoming call . . . from Angela Best. She apologised for the absence of her husband who had gone to have treatment for an ankle knock and then she passed the message: 'George wants to play for Hibs.'

Frankly, he would have been daft to turn them down. As Tom Hart announced the news, he pushed a slip of paper into my hand: 'That's what we are paying him – and it's confidential.'

Best was to be paid £2000 per game according to the scrawl of figures with an extra £2000 thrown in once he played a specific number of matches in succession.

I hurried off to the telephone to send what had turned out to be a smashing story while the other two prepared for the next stage.

D

We spent most of the day at quaint old Craven Cottage awaiting the arrival of Fulham manager Bobby Campbell to settle on a transfer fee. George owed the club some money and the deal worked out between £50,000 and £60,000.

Peter Marinello, who had been sold by Hibs to Arsenal, was on Fulham's books at the time, and a long chat with him helped to pass the time.

It was an odd transfer, really, with the principal character not even in attendance.

Two days later, Eddie Turnbull returned to London for Best's signature but George didn't think it was a good idea to make his debut against Celtic the following day and asked for another week to step up on his fitness.

So Bestie made his debut against St. Mirren at Love Street and the Paisley fans had never seen such a posse of press photographers. It was pandemonium behind the goal and also inside the tight confines of the pavilion with the superstar in demand.

It wasn't only the media who took an interest in Best, though, for the official gate was 13,670 – an instant tribute to the pulling power of one man.

Alas, the fairytale story did not produce the required ending except that George scored with a left-footed shot almost on the final whistle in a game Saints won 2-1.

Hibs still had only five points from 15 matches with a single victory against Dundee to show for the efforts of 23 players.

A special press conference had to be set up to allow Best to be photographed and interviewed about his new team, their prospects and the state of Scottish football in general. 'We're new to each other,' he said softly. 'And the lads are nervous in view of their League record.'

While everyone attached to the club suspected that Hibs were doomed for the drop, the arrival of Best had an extraordinary effect on the dressing-room morale. And those who questioned whether Tom Hart had taken a foolish gamble were amazed by the turn-out for George's first match at Easter Road against Partick Thistle.

Under normal circumstances, there might have been a gate of around 5000. But this was no normal occasion and 20,622 spectators were there to see the master in the flesh.

They weren't disappointed because Best cajoled his new colleagues into their first success for 14 weeks by the slender margin of 2-1. Goalkeeper Jim McArthur saved a penalty, Ally MacLeod scored one and an own goal by Brian Whittaker was enough to prompt celebrations.

Hibs were actually two goals ahead at half-time and should have coasted home, instead of which they were hanging on by their braces. George was delighted with the result and hoped his confidence could spread through the side. His passing had been spot-on and had drawn repeated bursts of applause from his fans.

The Irishman turned out in friendlies against Kilmarnock and Leicester and failed to appear for the next League game against Morton at Greenock. Tom Hart provided a cover story but was this the start of his tantrums?

Evidently not, for he shared in a 2-1 success over Rangers in the pre-Christmas match in which Tony Higgins and Colin Campbell scored goals, and he contributed a memorable goal in the drawn game with Celtic a fortnight later as 22,000 looked on.

February was a disastrous month for Best. He found time hanging heavily on his hands while he stayed alone in the North British Hotel, so he turned to drink.

Hibs suspended him for missing a fixture with Morton and eight days later, a few hours before a Sunday tie against Ayr United in the Scottish Cup, chairman Hart announced that the legendary winger was sacked.

He had gone on a three-day binge culminating in a party on the Saturday night with the Scotland and France rugby teams who had their post-international dinner in the same hotel.

Best was fast asleep when the Chairman called to see him, and disciplinary action was inevitable.

George flew home to London while Hibs qualified for the next round of the competition. It seemed he had shot himself in the foot once again.

But there was a lingering bond between the Hibs boardroom boss and the wayward wizard. Best admitted he was an alcoholic, started taking Antibuse tablets which would make him ill if he drank spirits, and Hibs offered to put him into a flat in Edinburgh with his wife.

Best tried hard and stuck to orange juice when he was in company. He went off to Portobello beach for runs along the sand to improve his condition. He played in eight more League games before the end of the season and in two Scottish Cup ties, including a semi final against Celtic.

One display stuck out above all others and that was a view of the vintage Best against Dundee at Easter Road. He scored a magnificent solo goal in a 2-0 win, dribbled as only he could and passed the ball to perfection. It was the best the fans had seen from a Hibs winger since the days of Gordon Smith.

But the team had only 14 points – all gained at Easter Road – and that was their total when Eddie Turnbull was dismissed on a Tuesday morning in mid-April after the semi-final thrashing from Celtic.

The late Willie Ormond became manager and Hibs won their first away point at Aberdeen. George was involved in a scuffle with Dons skipper Willie Miller in the tunnel as remarks were passed back and forward. Bestie was booked by referee David Murdoch and told Miller the lost point would cost them the title. It almost did but Aberdeen pipped Celtic by a point.

George had one more Premier League game against Dundee United as Hibs failed to move away from bottom spot in the table.

Hibs became the first Scottish club to introduce undersoil heating while the wandering genius went off to California for the summer sun.

But he was still on Hibs' books and reappeared in September to take part in four First Division matches and two League Cup ties, none of which were lost.

At Ayr, he played in Peter Cormack's boots after his own had gone astray on the train journey between Manchester and Glasgow, and his farewell appearance was against Falkirk on October 11. Hibs made him skipper for the day.

An agent had negotiated his transfer back to San Jose for the indoor season and the club recouped £30,000 of their initial outlay.

Despite his wayward tendencies, George remained big box office and he was popular with the players who sympathised with his goldfish-bowl existence.

Ralph Callachan, who invited George home for a meal one night before they attended a charity quiz, recalled the months in which they were teammates.

'It was quite difficult to get to know George when he was sometimes coming up at weekends to play. But the lads made him very welcome and we took him for a pint or a game of darts.'

'The big snag was that nobody would leave him alone. Fans wanted to chat or thrust bits of paper into his hand for an autograph. You had to feel sorry for him.'

'And then there was the day we witnessed the perfect set-up by a press photographer. There must have been 10 of us in the pub having a drink and that meant a whole lot of empty glasses.'

'This guy took a picture of George, looking totally disinterested, behind this table of empties and you can imagine how it looked in print. Someone might have wondered, though, why there was a kitty on the table.'

Ralph went on: 'George was a good lad – quiet but natural and we were pleasantly surprised by his whole attitude. Personally, I thought it was unfair that other players sometimes took stick for not linking up better with him. George would go off and have a game on his own which made it hard to play with him.'

'But he was great for us when things were going badly. He took all the pressure off us in that relegation season and it was a pleasure to play with him.'

I always found Best to be a charmer, gifted with the blarney if you like. However, he spoke nothing but the truth about his stay with Hibs: 'I thoroughly enjoyed it. Tom Hart did a lot for me and I'd like to think I repaid him for the faith he showed in me.'

Maybe he wasn't the Best I had seen beat Scotland single-handed with an astonishing virtuoso performance at Windsor Park in 1967. Or the young man whose extra-time trickery allowed Manchester United to become European champions in 1968 to fulfil an ambition for Matt Busby.

But he was still good value.

FULL IRISH HONOURS

1964

Apr.	Wales	(A) 3-2
Apr.	Uruguay	(H) 3-0
Oct.	England	(H) 3-4
Oct.	Switzerland	(H) 1-0
Nov.	Switzerland	(A) 1-2 (1)
Nov.	Scotland	(A) 2-3 (1)

1965

Mar.	Holland	(H) 2-1
Apr.	Holland	(A) 0-0
May	Albania	(H) 4-1 (1)
Oct.	Scotland	(H) 3-2
Nov.	England	(A) 1-2
Nov.	Albania	(A) 1-1

1966

Oct.	England	(H) 0-2

1967

Oct.	Scotland	(H) 1-0

1968

Oct.	Turkey	(H) 4-1

1969

May	England	(H) 1-3
May	Scotland	(A) 1-1
May	Wales	(H) 0-0
Sep.	Russia	(H) 0-0

1970

Apr.	Scotland	(H) 0-1
Apr.	England	(A) 1-3 (1)
Apr.	Wales	(A) 0-1
Nov.	Spain	(A) 0-3

1971

Feb.	Cyprus	(A) 3-0 (1)
Apr.	Cyprus	(H) 5-0 (3)
May	England	(H) 0-1
May	Scotland	(A) 1-0
May	Wales	(H) 1-0
Sep.	Russia	(A) 0-1

1972

Feb.	Spain	(H) 1-1
Oct.	Bulgaria	(A) 0-3

1973

Nov.	Portugal	(A) 1-1

1976

Oct.	Holland	(A) 2-2
Nov.	Belgium	(A) 0-2

1977

Apr.	West Germany	(A) 0-5
Sep.	Iceland	(H) 2-0
Oct.	Holland	(H) 0-1

Ireland score given first in every case

Alan Rough

There cannot be many international footballers who negotiated terms for a transfer at a boxing show but it was in these circumstances that Alan Rough signed for Hibs towards the end of November in 1982. Pat Stanton was the manager with the foresight to see that a class goalkeeper was necessary and started the ball rolling.

Alan received a telephone call from Partick Thistle asking him to report to Firhill earlier than usual at 5 pm. He arrived to learn from Peter Cormack that a fee had been agreed for his transfer and that the next stop was Edinburgh.

Pat was waiting at the Royal Scot Hotel and from there they travelled across the city to the Oratava Hotel, now converted into school buildings, to rendezvous with chairman Kenny Waugh whose love of boxing takes him to many local promotions.

A quick chat in a private room and the £65,000 deal was clinched in time to thrust Alan into a home debut against Celtic. Buying Scotland's most honoured goalkeeper proved to be one of the smartest transactions in Hibs' market moves though they had last-minute competition from Rangers.

John Greig reckoned the goalkeeper was great value and wanted to do business but there was no nod of approval from the Ibrox board and Rough fulfilled his ambition to belong to a full-time club by joining Hibs.

Not that he hadn't trained full-time at Firhill. He worked out three mornings each week with manager Cormack and also did three nights with the part-timers but Alan yearned for daily duty with a squad to maintain his edge.

He says: 'I'll always be indebted to Pat for signing me. I badly needed a move, having lost my Scotland place after the World Cup finals in Spain. He rescued my career and gave me fresh enthusiasm for the game.'

Alan had no qualms about flitting from his native Glasgow with his model wife, Michelle, and they hunted around East Lothian, eventually settling for a home in Gifford.

The big man who had been the international 'keeper for seven years became an instant hit with the Easter Road fans who needed a personality to lift a side with only seven points from a dozen matches.

Neither Rough nor two-goal Gary Murray could prevent a Celtic win by 3-2 in his first game but Alan quickly showed his value. Apart from a visit to Celtic Park where Hibs lost four goals, he was beaten only six times in 12 matches which produced 15 points and lifted the club out of the danger area.

Hibs finished eighth yet drew three times against Dundee United who won the championship by a point. Probably the most rewarding game for the supporters was the 8–1 destruction of Kilmarnock.

Willie Irvine's 14 goals before New Year kept Hibs in a respectable place in the following season and two of these goals were against Dundee at Dens Park where Alan had his name taken. He laughs when anyone reminds him of that yellow card: 'I was booked for time-wasting and it really was a joke when you consider we were three up and there were a couple of minutes to go.' Aberdeen referee Bill Knowles was the man with the sharp pencil.

Hibs required a run in the Scottish Cup to save the season but that competition turned into a disaster for the club and the goalkeeper. East Fife secured a gritty goalless draw at Easter Road and the replay at Bayview was going to be awkward on a chill January night on an icy pitch. Hibs were licked 2–0 and Alan was badly injured in the process.

Explained the 'keeper: 'My ankle was swollen and there was a lot of pain but the East Fife doctor examined me and confidently predicted there was no break and nothing to worry about.'

'I was still living in Glasgow at this time and drove home, hardly able to put my foot on the accelerator. I went to bed more hopeful than confident that I would be able to sleep. It was impossible, and in the early hours of the morning I rose and went to the Royal Infirmary for an X-ray.'

'What a dizzy at the hospital! They told me there was nobody on duty to take the X-rays and that I would have to return in the morning.'

'So, after a night of agony, it was back to hospital to learn that the ankle was broken and my mates at Easter Road were taken aback when I hobbled into the dressing room wearing a plaster.'

That post-match diagnosis at Methil had proved inaccurate and Alan could have avoided much discomfort by going straight to hospital for an examination.

It was two months on the sidelines and Hibs began to slip. Robin Rae took over in goal and the team collected only five points from nine games.

Alan was itching to play and pleaded with Pat to let him turn out against Dundee United reserves but he couldn't kick the ball and the idea was squashed.

Then, on the last day of March, there was an unexpected recall at Dundee though he was less than fit. Events of the previous night, outwith his knowledge, decreed that a Dens Park appearance was essential.

A reporter on the *Evening News* informed me early on the Saturday morning that a Hibs goalkeeper had been picked up by the police in the 'wee 'sma hours' and could face charges. The player in question was young Rae, and I rang Pat Stanton to see what he knew. 'Nothing' was the answer, and his thoughts turned immediately to his injured 'keeper.

Robin Rae was at the ground in time for the team bus and seemed surprised when the manager challenged him about being out late on the Friday night. Alan was surprised, too, when he learned of his selection.

His presence helped another victory through goals by Willie Jamieson and Wille Irvine, and only Celtic (yet again) beat Hibs in the remaining matches.

Although Rough was in splendid form for Hibs, his international days appeared to be over and he was constantly overlooked even as second choice. Still, Alan was not sore because he had enjoyed a long run as number one.

The early weeks of the '84–85 season brought no comfort to Hibs. A League Cup defeat by Meadowbank followed by a 3-2 home beating by Dumbarton in mid-September resulted in Pat Stanton's resignation.

Says Alan: 'I was sorry to see him go. He was my kind of manager and rather like myself as a laid-back individual. He had become totally frustated at the team's performace but I wish he had stayed on.'

Money can be found for a new manager and John Blackley, who had been assistant boss, was given the go-ahead to buy Gordon Durie from East Fife for another £65,000 within three weeks of taking over.

Tommy Craig was the next 'signing' from Carlisle as Blackley's right-hand man, a throwback to the friendship struck up during their Newcastle United days.

Durie was a powerfully built teenager with an eye for goal and he found himself with several new colleagues in the early weeks of the '85-86 campaign.

A Tribunal had decided that Nottingham Forest should pay £175,000 for Under-21 cap Brian Rice, and that windfall was used to finance signings.

Steve Cowan was purchased from Aberdeen to complement Durie, Mark Fulton switched from St. Mirren and Gordon Chisholm cost a reported £60,000 from Sunderland.

Hibs found their goals touch right away in the League Cup and Rough was little more than an onlooker as Durie and Cowan scored five each in the ties against Cowdenbeath and Motherwell.

Now it was Celtic at home on a Wednesday night and Alan was the hero of the game. Level at 3-3 after 90 minutes, the teams scored once each in extra time and so it went to penalties.

Alan didn't regard himself as an expert in these situations but he'll always remember that tie: 'I saved Celtic's first two penalties but Gordon Rae and Ally Brazil missed for us and we got through 3-2 when Pierce O'Leary put his effort over the bar.'

'Life was good at that point for I was recalled to the Scotland squad for the World Cup tie against Wales at Cardiff in the following week.'

That was to prove one of the most eventful games in Alan's life when he gained his 52nd cap at Ninian Park, and he relates the story: 'Wales led at half time with a Mark Hughes goal and the signs weren't hopeful that Scotland would gain the necessary point to qualify to play Australia for a World Cup place in Mexico.'

'At the interval, I went onto the park with the other substitutes to have a kickabout and enjoy some exercise. Suddenly, Brian Scott, the Celtic physiotherapist, came out of the dressing room and shouted that I was to go inside since I was on in the second half.'

'Now there is a lot of leg-pulling goes on between footballers and I felt sure this was another wind-up. I suggested to Brian that he should ask Jock Stein to come out in person and tell me there was to be a change.'

'Suddenly, I sensed there was no kidology and I hurried in to hear a brief message of 'You're on' from a manager who had been expressing his displeasure at the first-half display.'

'All my experience came in handy and I felt nerveless despite the atmosphere. The Welshmen didn't bother me much and the introduction of Davie Cooper in the last 20 minutes was a master stroke which enabled us to square the game through a penalty, from the sub.'

'But, of course, our delight soon turned to alarm at the finish when the players realised that Jock Stein had collapsed. We knew it was serious but we sat silent in the dressing room without any information about his condition.'

'Subsequently, we learned that the Big Man had died and it was a night I'll never forget. I think we spent two hours inside the Cardiff ground before anyone moved out, and we stayed in a state of shock on the flight home to Edinburgh.'

'People wanted to know why I had been introduced for Jim Leighton and I couldn't tell them. A story circulated that Jim had lost one of his contact lenses, and that came as a shock to me. I had roomed with him on international trips for a few years and had never seen him with any contacts.'

'George Wood, another Scotland goalkeeper, had worn them and I'd actually helped him to place or locate them in the past.'

Back on the home front, Hibs were due to face Rangers in the two-leg semi final of the League Cup with the first tie at Easter Road. Again Roughie starred by diving to stop a penalty from Ally McCoist, and goals by Durie and debutant Chisholm gave the side a winning lead.

Hibs soaked up the pressure at Ibrox where the unflappable goalkeeper was beaten only once and that result meant a final place against Aberdeen. John Blackley took his players to Ayrshire before the game and they trained on Irvine Meadow's pitch.

But Hibs were also-rans in the final and Alan says: 'Aberdeen were absolutely confident and knew how to handle the occasion. Our lads froze and never played at all. I suppose it makes a difference when you're accustomed to playing in finals. Gordon Rae's suspension didn't help, either.'

It was the same story in the Scottish Cup. After a thrilling home win against Celtic when Hibs turned round one down and won a magnificent game 4–3, Aberdeen barred the road to the final.

Dens Park was selected as the venue and if the ground had changed, the scoreline was the same and the Dons won 3–0. 'Just too good for us,' was how Roughie summed it up.

However, he had more excitement in store and yet another international appearance against England. With Leighton unfit, Alan was preferred to Andy Goram, possibly on account of his Wembley experience – and successes.

The famous London stadium might have been a graveyard for some Scottish goalkeepers but not for the Hibs man. He had been on winning sides there in 1977 and 1981 and was, in fact, hoping to complete a notable hat trick on England's home territory.

Unfortunately, it wasn't to be and Scotland lost 2–1 to ruin Alan's record. He told me: 'It was great to be at Wembley again but I hadn't expected to be picked. Alex Ferguson obviously had it in his mind to make Goram first reserve in the World Cup so why he wasn't given the chance, I'll never know.'

If the season was over for Hibs, there was no long summer break for Alan who was included in the Scotland pool for Mexico along with Leighton and Goram, but it didn't take him long to twig that he was only there as the third man!

'When we arrived at the Sheraton Hotel in Santa Fe for altitude training and I was allocated the single room while Jim and Andy shared a double, it was perfectly obvious where I stood in the ratings.'

'But being there almost in the role of a holidaymaker didn't bother me in the slightest. I had played in the finals in Argentina and Spain and it was my third World Cup. Not many players can say they've been involved in three finals.'

The New Mexico retreat was extremely pleasant and a sizeable Scottish colony did their best to make the squad feel at home. Alan was a spectator when the Scots had warm-up games in Los Angeles against Los Angeles Heat and Hollywood Kickers before flying into Mexico City and on to a country retreat in the middle of nowhere some miles outside the Capital. It certainly wasn't a patch on Santa Fe.

Alan has his own views about the World Cup finals in which Scotland lost to Denmark and West Germany and missed a chance to enter the quarter finals by the back door against Uruguay: 'I felt Alex Ferguson was overawed by the size of the competition, and he became more interested in trying to preserve a reasonable record as the team manager.'

'Alex was very pleasant to everyone during our month away and the Aberdeen players couldn't understand the change in his personality. He gave us nights out to break the monotony of training and his own Pittodrie lads said it was more his style to play the tough disciplinarian.'

'The soft shoe approach didn't work when Scotland were unable to beat Uruguay, who had 10 men after a first-minute foul on Gordon Strachan cost them a man, and obtained a goalless draw with ease.'

There was a sensational start to the season which began a few weeks after Argentina's triumph in Mexico. Rangers' new player-manager Graeme Souness was sent off for kicking Hibs centre forward George McCluskey in the Scotland captain's first club game in his native land at Easter Road.

Alan remained in his goalmouth as a free-for-all ensued in the centre circle and referee Delaney had great difficulty in sorting out the culprits from the innocent.

McCluskey was carried off with a gaping hole in his leg and some of the subsequent yellow cards might have been red. Roughie was booked in a separate incident and didn't necessarily agree with the decision.

Hibs won the all-ticket game 2–1 with goals from Stuart Beedie and Steve Cowan and the SFA swiftly set up an inquiry. Every player on the park during the fracas had two penalty points added to his disciplinary record – except Alan. Rangers were fined £5000 and Hibs £1000.

But the saga didn't end there, for three Hibs players took exception to the extra booking and submitted an appeal which was upheld on behalf of Mickey Weir, Mark Fulton and the injured McCluskey.

The resignation of manager John Blackley in mid-November drew these remarks from Alan. 'He was sometimes too hard – and on the wrong players. Perhaps he had tried to mould himself on Eddie Turnbull but, to me, John seemed to lack confidence in his own ability.'

Alex Miller's installation as boss resulted in improved protection for the goalkeeper and, consequently, fewer goals against Hibs. Easily the highlight of Rough's season was a glorious display in the 1–1 draw against Rangers at Ibrox where he broke the hearts of the home players until big Dave McPherson headed a late equaliser.

'I've always looked upon Ibrox as a lucky ground. While some players feel intimidated, I love the atmosphere and usually do well there.'

'It's the smaller grounds which are half empty that I dislike. John Blackley dropped me once after I had let in four goals at Cappielow which is not one of my favourite places.'

International statistics show that from Alan's first game against Switzerland in 1976 to his last appearance at Wembley in 1986, he conceded 63 goals at an average of 1.18 per game. He played in 24 winning teams and 18 that lost, having kept his goal intact in successive matches against England, Sweden and Ireland in 1981.

Alan was anxious to maintain his representative links and asked coach Andy Roxburgh if he could lend his experience to the senior side or else help with the Under 19s but the offer was refused.

Glasgow-born in 1951, Alan plans to play on for some years and is, in fact, under contract to Hibs until 1989. Apart from his cap collection, he won a League Cup badge with Partick Thistle in that famous final of 1971 when Celtic were supposed to walk-over, and is an ex-Scotland Player of the Year.

He would like to feature in a winning Hibs team against Hearts after several seasons of derby disappointments and, with his wife Michelle and son Alan, he is keeping a watchful eye on Jim Leighton's appearances for Scotland and chuckles: 'Jim has passed Bill Brown's total but he has some way to go yet to draw alongside mine.'

FULL INTERNATIONAL CAPS

1976

Apr.	Switzerland	(H) 1-0
May	Wales	(H) 3-1
May	Ireland	(H) 3-0
May	England	(H) 2-1
Sep.	Finland	(H) 6-0
Oct.	Czechoslovakia	(A) 0-2
Nov.	Wales	(H) 1-0

1977

Apr.	Sweden	(H) 3-1
May	Wales	(A) 0-0
June	Ireland	(H) 3-0
June	England	(A) 2-1
June	Chile	(A) 4-2
June	Argentina	(A) 1-1
June	Brazil	(A) 0-2
Sep.	Czechoslovakia	(H) 3-1
Oct.	Wales	(A) 2-0

1978

May	Ireland	(H) 1-1
May	England	(H) 0-1
June	Peru	(A) 1-3
June	Iran	(A) 1-1
June	Holland	(A) 3-2
Sep.	Austria	(A) 2-3
Nov.	Portugal	(A) 0-1

1979

May	Wales	(A) 0-3
June	Argentina	(H) 1-3
June	Norway	(A) 4-0
Sep.	Peru	(H) 1-1
Oct.	Austria	(H) 1-1
Nov.	Belgium	(A) 0-2
Dec.	Belgium	(H) 1-3

1980

Mar.	Portugal	(H) 4-1
May	Wales	(H) 1-0
May	England	(H) 0-2
May	Poland	(A) 0-1
May	Hungary	(A) 1-3
Sep.	Sweden	(A) 1-0
Oct.	Portugal	(H) 0-0

1981

Feb.	Israel	(A) 1-0
Mar.	Ireland	(H) 1-1
Apr.	Israel	(H) 3-1
May	Wales	(A) 0-2
May	England	(A) 1-0
Sep.	Sweden	(H) 2-0
Oct.	Ireland	(A) 0-0

1982		
Feb.	Spain	(A) 0-3
Mar.	Holland	(H) 2-1
May	Wales	(H) 1-0
May	England	(H) 0-1
June	New Zealand	(A) 5-2
June	Brazil	(A) 1-4
June	Russia	(A) 2-2

1985		
*Sep.	Wales	(A) 1-1
1986		
Apr.	England	(A) 1-2

* substitute

The Scotland score is given first in every case

Championship Points — '46 to '87

YEAR	PLACE	GAMES	POINTS
1947	2nd	30	44
1948	1st	30	48
1949	3rd	30	39
1950	2nd	30	49
1951	1st	30	48
1952	1st	30	45
1953	2nd	30	43
1954	5th	30	34
1955	5th	30	34
1956	4th	34	45
1957	9th	34	33
1958	9th	34	31
1959	11th	34	32
1960	7th	34	35
1961	7th	34	34
1962	8th	34	33
1963	16th	34	25
1964	10th	34	30
1965	4th	34	46
1966	6th	34	38
1967	5th	34	42
1968	3rd	34	45
1969	12th	34	31
1970	3rd	34	44
1971	12th	34	30
1972	4th	34	44
1973	3rd	34	45
1974	2nd	34	49
1975	2nd	34	49
1976	3rd	36	43
1977	6th	36	34
1978	4th	36	37
1979	5th	36	37
1980*	10th	36	18
1981†	1st	39	57
1982	6th	36	36
1983	7th	36	29
1984	7th	36	31
1985	8th	36	27
1986	8th	36	28
1987	9th	44	33

*Relegated †Promoted

Scottish Cup Record

1924-25	1st rd:	Hibs v Aberdeen 0-2
1925-26	1st rd:	Hibs v Broxburn United 1-1, 1-0
	2nd rd:	Hibs v Airdrie 2-3
1926-27	1st rd:	Cowdenbeath v Hibs 3-0
1927-28	1st rd:	Hibs (*w.o.*) v Dykehead (*scr.*)
	2nd rd:	Third Lanark v Hibs 0-2
	3rd rd:	Hibs v Falkirk 0-0, 1-0
	4th rd:	Dunfermline v Hibs 0-4
	Semi:	Hibs v Rangers 0-3
1928-29	1st rd:	Hibs v St. Johnstone 1-2
1929-30	1st rd:	Hibs v Leith Amateurs 2-0
	2nd rd:	Ayr United v Hibs 1-3
	3rd rd:	Hibs v Hearts 1-3
1930-31	1st rd:	Hibs v St. Cuthbert's 3-1
	2nd rd:	Hamilton v Hibs 2-2, 2-5
	3rd rd:	Hibs v Motherwell 0-3
1931-32	1st rd:	Hibs v Dundee United 2-3
1932-33	1st rd:	Hibs v Forfar Athletic 2-2, 7-3
	2nd rd:	Aberdeen v Hibs 1-1, 0-1
	3rd rd:	Bye
	4th rd:	Hibs v Hearts 0-0, 0-2
1933-34	1st rd:	Hibs v Clyde 5-4
	2nd rd:	Hibs v Alloa 6-0
	3rd rd:	Hibs v Aberdeen 0-1
1934-35	1st rd:	Hibs v Vale of Atholl 5-0
	2nd rd:	Hibs v Clachnacuddin 7-1
	3rd rd:	Aberdeen v Hibs 0-0, 1-1, 3-2
1935-36	1st rd:	Vale Acoba v Hibs 1-3
	2nd rd:	Clyde v Hibs 4-1

1936-37	1st rd: Alloa v Hibs 2-5
	2nd rd: Hamilton Acad. v Hibs 2-1
1937-38	1st rd: Hibs v Edinburgh City 2-3
1938-39	1st rd: Forfar v Hibs 0-3
	2nd rd: Hibs v Kilmarnock 3-1
	3rd rd: Bye
	4th rd: Hibs v Alloa Athletic 3-1
	Semi: Hibs v Clyde 0-1
1939-46	*No Competition*
1946-47	1st rd: Alloa v Hibs 0-8
	2nd rd: Bye
	3rd rd: Rangers v Hibs 0-0, 0-2
	4th rd: Hibs v Dumbarton 2-0
	Semi: Hibs v Motherwell 2-1
	Final (Hampden): Hibs v Aberdeen 1-2
1947-48	1st rd: Albion Rovers v Hibs 0-2
	2nd rd: Hibs v Arbroath 4-0
	3rd rd: Hibs v Aberdeen 4-2
	4th rd: Hibs v St. Mirren 3-1
	Semi: Rangers v Hibs 1-0
1948-49	1st rd: Forfar Ath. v Hibs 0-4
	2nd rd: Hibs v Raith Rovers 1-1, 4-3
	3rd rd: Bye
	4th rd: Hibs v East Fife 0-2
1949-50	1st rd: Hibs v Partick Thistle 0-1
1950-51	1st rd: St. Mirren v Hibs 1-1, 0-5
	2nd rd: Bye
	3rd rd: Rangers v Hibs 2-3
	4th rd: Airdrie v Hibs 0-3
	Semi: Hibs v Motherwell 2-3
1951-52	1st rd: Raith Rovers v Hibs 0-0, 0-0, 4-1
1952-53	1st rd: Hibs v Stenhousemuir 8-1
	2nd rd: Hibs v Queen's Park 4-2
	3rd rd: Airdrie v Hibs 0-4
	4th rd: Hibs v Aberdeen 1-1, 0-2

1953-54	1st rd:	St. Johnstone v Hibs 1-2
	2nd rd:	Hibs v Clyde 7-0
	3rd rd:	Hibs v Aberdeen 1-3
1954-55	5th rd:	Hearts v Hibs 5-0
1955-56	5th rd:	Hibs v Raith Rovers 1-1, 1-3
1956-57	5th rd:	Hibs v Aberdeen 3-4
1957-58	1st rd:	Bye
	2nd rd:	Dundee Utd. v Hibs 0-0, 0-2
	3rd rd:	Hearts v Hibs 3-4
	4th rd:	Hibs v Third Lanark 3-2
	Semi:	Rangers v Hibs 2-2, 1-2
	Final	(Hampden): Clyde v Hibs 1-0
1958-59	1st rd:	Raith Rovers v Hibs 1-1, 1-2
	2nd rd:	Hibs v Falkirk 3-1
	3rd rd:	Hibs v Partick Thistle 4-1
	4th rd:	Third Lanark v Hibs 2-1
1959-60	2nd rd:	Hibs v Dundee 3-0
	3rd rd:	East Stirling v Hibs 0-3
	4th rd:	Rangers v Hibs 3-2
1960-61	1st rd:	Clyde v Hibs 0-2
	2nd rd:	Hibs v Peebles 15-1
	3rd rd:	Hamilton v Hibs 0-4
	4th rd:	Celtic v Hibs 1-1, 1-0
1961-62	1st rd:	Partick Thistle v Hibs 2-2, 3-2
1962-63	2nd rd:	Brechin v Hibs 0-2
	3rd rd:	Dundee v Hibs 1-0
1963-64	1st rd:	Aberdeen v Hibs 5-2
1964-65	1st rd:	Hibs v E.S. Clydebank 1-1, 2-0
	2nd rd:	Hibs v Partick Thistle 5-1
	3rd rd:	Hibs v Rangers 2-1
	Semi:	Hibs v Dunfermline 0-2
1965-66	1st rd:	Hibs v Third Lanark 4-3
	2nd rd:	Hearts v Hibs 2-1

1966-67	1st rd:	Hibs v Brechin City 2-0
	2nd rd:	Hibs v Berwick Rangers 1-0
	3rd rd:	Hibs v Aberdeen 1-1, 0-3
1967-68	1st rd:	East Stirling v Hibs 3-5
	2nd rd:	Airdrie v Hibs 1-0
1968-69	1st rd:	Rangers v Hibs 1-0
1969-70	1st rd:	Rangers v Hibs 3-1
1970-71	1st rd:	Hibs v Forfar 8-1
	2nd rd:	Hearts v Hibs 1-2
	3rd rd:	Hibs v Dundee 1-0
	Semi:	Hibs v Rangers 0-0, 1-2
1971-72	1st rd:	Partick Thistle v Hibs 0-2
	2nd rd:	Hibs v Airdrie 2-0
	3rd rd:	Hibs v Aberdeen 2-0
	Semi:	Hibs v Rangers 1-1, 2-0
	Final:	Hibs v Celtic 1-6
1972-73	1st rd:	Hibs v Morton 2-0
	2nd rd:	Rangers v Hibs 1-1, 2-1
1973-74	1st rd:	Hibs v Kilmarnock 5-2
	2nd rd:	St. Johnstone v Hibs 0-3
	3rd rd:	Hibs v Dundee 3-3, 0-3
1974-75	1st rd:	Hibs 0, Celtic 2
1975-76	1st rd:	Hibs 3, Dunfermline 2
	2nd rd:	Hibs 1, Dundee United 1
	Replay:	Dundee United 0, Hibs 2
	3rd rd:	Motherwell 2, Hibs 2
	Replay:	Hibs 1, Motherwell 1 (after extra time)
	Replay:	Hibs 1, Motherwell 2 (at Ibrox)
1976-77	1st rd:	Hibs 3, Partick Thistle 0
	2nd rd:	Arbroath 1, Hibs 1
	Replay:	Hibs 1, Arbroath 2
1977-78	1st rd:	Hibs 4, East Fife 0
	2nd rd:	Hibs 0, Partick Thistle 0
	Replay:	Partick Thistle 2, Hibs 1

1978-79	1st rd:	Dunfermline 1, Hibs 1
	Replay:	Hibs 2, Dunfermline 0
	2nd rd:	Meadowbank 0, Hibs 6 (at Easter Road)
	3rd rd:	Hibs 2, Hearts 1
	Semi:	Hibs 2, Aberdeen 1 (at Hampden)
	Final:	Hibs 0, Rangers 0 (at Hampden)
	Replay:	Hibs 0, Rangers 0 (after extra time at Hampden)
	Replay:	Hibs 2, Rangers 3 (after extra time at Hampden)
1979-80	1st rd:	Meadowbank 0, Hibs 1 (at Tynecastle)
	2nd rd:	Hibs 2, Ayr United 0
	3rd rd:	Berwick 0, Hibs 0
	Replay:	Hibs 1, Berwick 0
	Semi:	Hibs 0, Celtic 5 (at Hampden)
1980-81	1st rd:	Hibs 1, Dunfermline 1
	Replay:	Dunfermline 1, Hibs 2
	2nd rd:	Hibs 1, Falkirk 0
	3rd rd:	Rangers 3, Hibs 1
1981-82	1st rd:	Hibs 2, Falkirk 0
	2nd rd:	Dundee United 1, Hibs 1
	Replay:	Hibs 1, Dundee United 1
	Replay:	Hibs 0, Dundee United 3 (at Easter Road)
1982-83	1st rd:	Hibs 1, Aberdeen 4
1983-84	1st rd:	Hibs 0, East Fife 0
	Replay:	East Fife 2, Hibs 0
1984-85	1st rd:	Dundee United 3, Hibs 0
1985-86	1st rd:	Hibs 2, Dunfermline 0
	2nd rd:	Hibs 1, Ayr 0
	3rd rd:	Hibs 4, Celtic 3
	Semi:	Hibs 0, Aberdeen 3 (at Dens Park)
1986-87	1st rd:	Hibs 2, Dunfermline 0
	2nd rd:	Clydebank 1, Hibs 0

LEAGUE CUP RECORD

1946-47—Won section with Celtic, Hamilton, Kilmarnock. Quarter final—Airdrie (a) 4-4; Airdrie (h) 1-0, after extra time. Semi-final—Rangers (Hampden) 1-3.

1947-48—Did not qualify in section with Hearts, Airdrie, Clyde.

1948-49—Did not qualify in section with Rangers, Celtic, Clyde.

1949-50—Won section with Falkirk, Third Lanark, Queen of South. Quarter final—Partick Thistle (a) 2-4; Partick Thistle (h) 4-0. Semi-final—Dunfermline (Tynecastle) 1-2.

1950-51—Won section with Dundee, Falkirk, St. Mirren. Quarter final—Aberdeen (a) 1-4; Aberdeen (h) 4-1. Replay—Aberdeen (Ibrox) 1-1; Second replay—Aberdeen (Hampden) 5-1. Semi-final—Queen of South (Tynecastle) 3-1. FINAL—Motherwell (Hampden) 0-3.

1951-52—Did not qualify in section with Motherwell, Partick Thistle, Stirling Albion.

1952-53—Won section with Celtic, Partick Thistle, St. Mirren. Quarter final—Morton (a) 6-0; Morton (h) 6-3. Semi final—Dundee (Tynecastle) 1-2.

1953-54—Won section with Queen of South, Falkirk, St. Mirren. Quarter final—Third Lanark (a) 4-0; Third Lanark (h) 4-0. Semi final—East Fife (Tynecastle) 2-3.

1954-55—Did not qualify in section with Aberdeen, East Fife, Queen of South.

1955-56—Did not qualify in section with Aberdeen, Dunfermline, Clyde.

1956-57—Did not qualify in section with Partick Thistle, Falkirk, Hearts.

1957-58—Did not qualify in section with Celtic, Airdrie, East Fife.

1958-59—Did not qualify in section with Falkirk, Aberdeen, Kilmarnock.

1959-60—Did not qualify in section with Motherwell, Dundee, Rangers.

1960-61—Did not qualify in section with Kilmarnock, Dunfermline, Airdrie.

1961-62—Did not qualify in section with St. Johnstone, Partick Thistle, Celtic.

1962-63—Did not qualify in section with Rangers, St. Mirren, Third Lanark.

1963-64—Won section with St. Mirren, Aberdeen, Dundee United. Quarter final—Dundee (a) 3-3; Dundee (h) 2-0. Semi final—Morton (Ibrox) 1-1; replay—Morton (Ibrox) 0-1.

1964-65—Did not qualify in section with Third Lanark, Dunfermline, Airdrie.

1965-66—Won section with Falkirk, St. Mirren, Morton. Quarter final—Alloa (a) 2-0; Alloa (h) 11-2. Semi final—Celtic (Ibrox) 2-2; Celtic (Ibrox) 0-4.

1966-67—Did not qualify in section with Rangers, Kilmarnock, Stirling Albion.

1967-68—Did not qualify in section with Dundee, Motherwell, Clyde.

1968-69—Won section with St. Johnstone, Raith Rovers, Partick Thistle. Quarter final—East Fife (a) 4-1; East Fife (h) 2-1. Semi final—Dundee (Tynecastle) 2-1. FINAL—Celtic (Hampden) 2-6.

1969-70—Did not qualify in section with Clyde, Dunfermline, Aberdeen.

1970-71—Won section with St. Johnstone, Airdrie, Aberdeen. Quarter final—Rangers (h) 1-3; Rangers (a) 1-3.

1971-72—Won section with Motherwell, Kilmarnock, Dundee United. Quarter final—Falkirk (a) 0-2; Falkirk (h) 1-0.

1972-73—Qualified in section with Aberdeen, Queen's Park, Queen of South. First round—Dundee United (a) 5-2; Dundee United (h) 0-0. Second round—Airdrie (a) 6-2; Airdrie (h) 4-1. Semi final—Rangers (Hampden) 1-0. FINAL—Celtic (Hampden) 2-1.

1973-74—Won section with Morton, Ayr United, Dumbarton. First round—Raith Rovers (h) 3-2; Raith Rovers (a) 2-0. Second round—Rangers (a) 0-2; Rangers (h) 0-0.

1974-75—Qualified in section with Rangers, Dundee and St. Johnstone. Quarter final—Kilmarnock (a) 3-3; Kilmarnock (h) 4-1; Semi final in Falkirk (Tynecastle) 1-0; FINAL Celtic (Hampden) 3-6.

1975-76—Qualified in section with Dundee, Ayr and Dunfermline. Quarter final in Montrose (h) 1-0; Montrose (a) 1-3 after extra time.

1976-77—Did not qualify in section with Rangers, Montrose and St. Johnstone.

1977-78—First round—Queen of South (h) 1-2; Queens of South (a) 0-0.

1978-79—First round—Brechin (a) 3-0; Brechin (h) 3-1; Second round—Clydebank (h) 1-0; Clydebank (a) 1-1; Third round—Morton (a) 0-1; Morton (h) 2-0; Semi final—Aberdeen 0-1 at Dens Park.

1979-80—First round—Montrose (h) 2-1; Montrose (a) 1-1; Second round in Kilmarnock (h) 1-2; Kilmarnock (a) 1-2.

1980-81—First round—Alloa (a) 2-0; Alloa (h) 1-1; Second round—Clyde (a) 2-0; Clyde (h) 2-1; Third round—Ayr (a) 2-2; Ayr (h) 0-2 after extra time.

1981-82—Did not qualify in section with Celtic, St. Mirren and St. Johnstone.

1982-83—Failed to qualify in section with Rangers, Clydebank and Airdrie.

1983-84—Preliminary round in Dumbarton (h) 5-0; Dumbarton (a) 2-1. Failed to qualify in section with Kilmarnock, Celtic and Airdrie.

1984-85—First round—East Fife (h) 1-0; Second round—Meadowbank (h) 1-2 (after extra time).

1985-86—First round—Cowdenbeath (h) 6-0; Second round—Motherwell (h) 6-1; Third round—Celtic (h) 4-4 (won on penalties after extra time); Semi final—Rangers (h) 2-0; Rangers (a) 0-1. FINAL—Aberdeen 0-3 at Hampden.

1986-87—First round—East Stirling (h) 1-0; Second round—Hamilton (a) 1-0; Third round—Dundee United (h) 0-2.

European Record

European Cup

1955-56

Rd. 1	Rot Weiss Essen	(A)	4-0	Turnbull 2, Reilly, Ormond.
Rd. 1	Rot Weiss Essen	(H)	1-1	J. Buchanan.
Rd. 2	Djurgaarden	(H)	1-0	Turnbull, pen.
Rd. 2	Djurgaarden	(A)	3-1	Turnbull, pen., Combe, Mulkerrin.
SF	Rheims	(A)	0-2	

Fairs Cup

1960-61

Rd. 2	Barcelona	(A)	4-4	Baker 2, Preston, Macleod.
Rd. 2	Barcelona	(H)	3-2	Baker, Preston, Kinloch, pen.
SF	Roma	(H)	2-2	Baker, Macleod.
SF	Roma	(A)	3-3	Baker 2, Kinloch.
SF	Roma	(A)	0-6	

1961-62

Rd. 1	Belenenses	(H)	3-3	Fraser 2, Baird, pen.
Rd. 1	Belenenses	(A)	3-1	Baxter 2, Stevenson.
Rd. 2	Red Star	(A)	0-4	
Rd. 2	Red Star	(H)	0-1	

1962-63

Rd. 1 Copenhagen.................. (H) 4-0 Byrne, G. Baker, M. Stevenson, o.g.
Rd. 1 Copenhagen.................. (A) 3-2 M. Stevenson 2, Byrne.
Rd. 2 Utrecht.............................. (A) 1-0 Falconer.
Rd. 2 Utrecht.............................. (H) 2-1 G. Baker, M. Stevenson.
Rd. 3 Valencia........................... (A) 0-5
Rd. 3 Valencia........................... (H) 2-1 G. Baker, Preston.

1965-66

Rd. 1 Valencia........................... (H) 2-0 McNamee, Scott.
Rd. 1 Valencia........................... (A) 0-2
Rd. 1 Valencia........................... (A) 0-3

1967-68

Rd. 1 Porto .... (H) 3-0 Cormack 2, Stevenson.
Rd. 1 Porto .... (A) 1-3 Davis, pen.
Rd. 2 Naples .... (A) 1-4 Stein.
Rd. 2 Naples .... (H) 5-0 R. Duncan, Quinn, Cormack, Stanton, Stein.

Rd. 3 Leeds United .... (A) 0-1
Rd. 3 Leeds United .... (H) 1-1 Stein.

1968-69

Rd. 1 Olympia .... (A) 3-0 Stevenson, Stein, o.g.
Rd. 1 Olympia .... (H) 2-1 Davis 2 pens.
Rd. 2 Lokomotive Leipzig ..... (H) 3-1 McBride 3.
Rd. 2 Lokomotive Leipzig ..... (A) 1-0 Grant.
Rd. 3 Hamburg .... (A) 0-1
Rd. 3 Hamburg .... (H) 2-1 McBride 2.

1970-71

Rd. 1 Malmo .... (H) 6-0 McBride 3, Duncan 2, Blair.
Rd. 1 Malmo .... (A) 3-2 Stanton, McEwan, R. Duncan.
Rd. 2 Guimaraes...................... (H) 2-0 Stanton, Duncan.
Rd. 2 Guimaraes...................... (A) 1-2 Graham.
Rd. 3 Liverpool......................... (H) 0-1
Rd. 3 Liverpool......................... (A) 0-2

Cup Winners Cup

1972-73

Rd. 1 Sporting .... (A) 1-2 Duncan.
Rd. 1 Sporting .... (H) 6-1 O'Rourke 3, Gordon, 2, o.g.
Rd. 2 F.C. Besa .... (H) 7-1 O'Rourke 3, Duncan 2, Cropley, Brownlie.
Rd. 2 F.C. Besa .... (A) 1-1 Gordon.
Rd. 3 Hajduk Split .... (H) 4-2 Gordon 3, Duncan.
Rd. 3 Hajduk Split .... (A) 0-3

UEFA Cup

1973-74

Rd. 1 Keflavik.......................... (H) 2-0
Rd. 1 Keflavik.......................... (A) 1-1
Rd. 2 Leeds United .... (A) 0-0
Rd. 2 Leeds United .... (H) 0-0 Hibs beaten 5-4 on penalties.

1974-75

Rd. 1 Rosenborg..................... (A) 3-2 Stanton, Cropley, Gordon.
Rd. 1 Rosenborg..................... (H) 9-1 Stanton 2, Cropley 2 pens, Harper 2, Munro 2, Gordon.
Rd. 2 Juventus .... (H) 2-4 Stanton, Cropley
Rd. 2 Juventus .... (A) 0-4

1975-76

Rd. 1 Liverpool........................ (H) 1-0 Harper
Rd. 1 Liverpool........................ (A) 1-3 Edwards

1976-77

Rd. 1 Sochaux........................ (H) 1-0 Brownlie
Rd. 1 Sochaux........................ (A) 0-0
Rd. 2 Oesters.......................... (H) 2-0 Blackley, Brownlie pen.
Rd. 2 Oesters.......................... (A) 1-4 Smith

1978-79

Rd. 1 Norrkoping.................... (H) 3-2 Higgins 2, Temperley
Rd. 1 Norrkoping.................... (A) 0-0
Rd. 2 Strasbourg .... (A) 0-2
Rd. 2 Strasbourg .... (H) 1-0 MacLeod, pen.